# Lotus

## DEPRESSION GLASS & FAR BEYOND

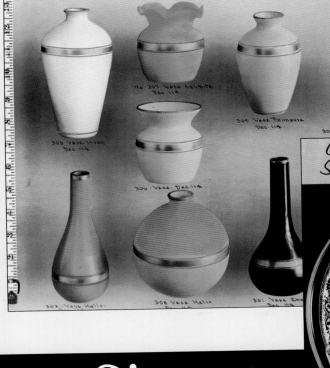

Schiffer Publishing Ltd®

-880 Lower Valley Road, Atglen, PA 19310 USA

# Dean Six

To Bob & Dale – there is no price guide for friendship.

Designed by Mark David Bowyer
Type set in Zapf Chancery Bd BT/Aldine 721 BT

ISBN: 0-7643-2163-3
ed in China

Published by Schiffer Publishing Ltd.
4880 Lower Valley Road
Atglen, PA 19310
Phone: (610) 593-1777; Fax: (610) 593-2002
E-mail: Info@schifferbooks.com

For the largest selection of fine reference books on this and related subjects, please visit our web site at **www.schifferbooks.com**
We are always looking for people to write books on new and related subjects. If you have an idea for a book please contact us at the above address.

This book may be purchased from the publisher.
Include $3.95 for shipping.
Please try your bookstore first.
You may write for a free catalog.

In Europe, Schiffer books are distributed by
Bushwood Books
6 Marksbury Ave.
Kew Gardens
Surrey TW9 4JF England
Phone: 44 (0) 20 8392-8585; Fax: 44 (0) 20 8392-9876
E-mail: info@bushwoodbooks.co.uk
Free postage in the U.K., Europe; air mail at cost.

# Contents

# A Chapter of Thanks

With each book project I undertake I realize more fully and appreciate how many people really write any book. Yet a single author's name is generally put forth. While my name is here, others share the credit for making this project a reality. While this may read a bit like an Oscar acceptance speech, it is, none the less, true.

Bob Page and Dale Fredericksen, my friends of many years, took an interest in Lotus long ago and created the first and only prior book addressing the company or ware. Their book, *A Collection of American Crystal* (Greensboro, North Carolina: Page-Fredericksen Publishing Co., 1995), addressed three major American glass decorators and Lotus was one of the chosen. More importantly, in preparing their work for publication they acquired a significant collection of Lotus Glass Company archival material. While this work is not exclusively drawn from that body of material, it is based heavily and predominately upon that major, single source. Simply and honestly, there would be no Lotus book from me were it not for their willingness to share the information they gathered some years ago. How can one say thanks to that? For myself and for the hundreds and thousands of users of this work in the years to come, a sincere Thank You to Bob and Dale for their nearly endless support of this and countless other good works. To any reader it will be their prior book that is and will remain the definitive book on the expansive Lotus decorated stemware and stem identification. I urge your consideration of their book *A Collection of American Crystal* for your bookshelf.

The Hanse family, long time owners of Lotus Glass, welcomed my inquiries warmly and shared from their family collection of archival material. Many photos and some of the product illustrations appearing here were kindly shared by Don Hanse.

Hazel Marie Weatherman, the leader in writing and documenting depression era glass, lifted Lotus as a company from possible oblivion when she included it in her major and yet today exceedingly useful work, *Colored Glassware of the Depression Era 2*, published in 1974. Literally hundreds of other companies, glass producers, and decorators have faded from memory and their stories will likely never be told. With Weatherman's inserting this one decorating firm amidst the mass of other hot glass producers, Lotus first claimed its place in history. I suggest that today, a quarter of a century after she wrote it, few books are as useful as her *Depression 2* book. It should be in every glass library.

My additional personal thanks for support on this project go to:

Tom & Neila Bredehoft
Tom Felt
Jaime Robinson
Deshond McGee
Tim Schmidt
Ralph & Eleanor Six
Helen Jones
Don Hanse
Rick Hanse

# Chapter One

# History of Lotus

In early twentieth century America, the culture of change was upon us. As the twentieth century unfolded, Americans were discovering mass-produced Model T automobiles, hearing about aeroplane flights, and beginning to listen to their wireless sets—the device that would become today's radio. Americans were becoming accustomed to a world where the concepts of new and changing would become an ever more important part of culture.

Material culture, the objects, designs, fashions, and fads that surround us, would be the vanguard for the expanding society of change seekers. Within that material culture, the decorative arts, not the least being glass, would take a visible role. We, as Americans, would grow to define ourselves more and more by the objects we owned. The task of seeking and acquiring those objects, the concepts of shopping, marketing, and advertising were emerging from their infancy. It was into this new world and young century that Lotus Cut Glass Company opened in Barnesville, Ohio, in 1912. Success may have come early as a new factory was constructed in 1915 on Mulberry Street, near the railroad depot, that would serve the company for decades.

The new factory constructed in 1915 on Mulberry Street. Photo by W. Baker. Hanse family collection.

A view inside the factory on Mulberry Street showing a cutting room with the overhead power drives and funnels to provide dripping water to fast turning cutting wheels and ware. Note the use of natural light in a time when electric light was not yet readily available. Circa 1920. Photo by W. Baker. Hanse family collection.

Lotus began as Lotus Cut Glass Company and expanded within the next decade to incorporate other manners of decoration into their product line. Noteworthy is the use of the descriptive Cut Glass in the original name, for the company was formed to decorate by cutting and not to manufacture glass. At no time in its decades long history did Lotus produce the glass blanks upon which they created their magic. Lotus was not a hot glass factory. For simplification, I suggest we think of Lotus as the artists whose creations, sometimes literally paintings, are placed upon the unadorned blanks crafted by others. Imagine acquiring canvases to paint upon and that was the Lotus relationship to the almost endless list of suppliers of unadorned glass for Lotus to decorate. The list of supplier of blanks to Lotus is in itself impressive and is addressed in a list near the end of this chapter.

The story of Lotus becomes the story of the Hanse family over time. Matthew Hanse, a glass cutter, was one of the original employees of Lotus Cut Glass and in 1913 became plant superintendent. Hanse later became a stockholder, plant manager, and later still held controlling interest in the company. In 1924, the firm changed its name from Lotus Cut Glass to Lotus Glass, better reflecting their diversity of decorating techniques then used. The *Crockery & Glass Journal*, August 28, 1924, tells us that when the company was formed, "light cut glass formed the entire production of the factory. During the years that followed, the glass market changed, as well a methods of production, and the concern's line was built up to include a variety of attractive items in a general line of cut, plate etched, and decorated glassware. In addition to this the concern are now decorating fine imported china. This expansion was in addition to a large cut glass business the company enjoyed. The word 'Cut' in the corporate title of this company has not expressed the real importance of the line to the glass trade, and in realizing this, the stockholders authorized the change."

In 1928, the process described by the Hanse family as "silver plating" or silver decorating was begun as a part of the Lotus line. By 1943, cutting as a decorative treatment remained popular enough that the company opened a second cutting shop. This was in part due to the lack of imports for American tableware during World War II. The application by hand of 22 and 24 karat gold was a long time successful Lotus technique that ended in 1980 when the "long time employee who mixed the gold died."

The 1920s were a roaring time in the US, and for Lotus it appears. Shown here in a 1928 ad is Gothic Plantagonet, an elaborate glass decorating *tour de force*.

Silver Deposit decoration was introduced at Lotus in 1928. This undated ad from the *Crockery & Glass Journal* touts Sterling Silver on jade green glass.

Prosperous Lotus Glass sporting a new company vehicle in 1929. H.D. Burkhead, sales representative, beside the vehicle with the factory in the background. Hanse family collection.

Decoration on glass was not the only undertaking from Lotus. They decorated fine china for a period early in the twentieth century. Perhaps it was later that Lotus also tried their hand at decorating Art Pottery with silver deposit. Sometime circa 1940s Lotus was the sole U.S. distributor of Royal Blue Delft pottery from Holland as well, further exploring china and glass avenues for their emerging company.

A Lotus catalog photograph illustrating Bavarian China Service plates, heavily etched and gold encrusted. Lotus experimented with numerous lines in addition to glass. Circa 1920s.

In addition to efforts at fine china, Lotus decorated art pottery sometime circa late 1920s.
Here are examples of their Sterling Silver creations. Who would have ever attributed these
products to Lotus Glass of Barnesville, Ohio, were it not for this two fold brochure?

Upon Matthew (M.A.) Hanse's passing in 1968, it was his son, Francis, who assumed the presidency of Lotus. Francis himself was far from a stranger to the works of Lotus, having been employed there since 1938 and appointed treasurer and sales manager in 1946.

One of several peaks for Lotus was the post World War II era when service men returning home to establish families boomed the market for American made housewares. The finely decorated products of Lotus won approval across the country and many a mid-century bride chose a Lotus crystal pattern for her new life and home. In Barnesville employment at Lotus stabilized at over 100 employees, with some reports suggesting 200 people were engaged at Lotus at the peak. In the 1930-50s era, Lotus had close working relationships with Louie Glass in Weston, West Virginia, according to Don Hanse. However, Hanse added, that when items were needed and Louie could not meet the demand in a timely manner, it was not uncommon to "run to Mid-Atlantic Glass or Jane Lew to get something made."

The practice of shopping for the most affordable blank seemed to prevail at Lotus as it did within the industry at large. One unexpected note learned from Don Hanse was that Lotus owned their own glass molds for some shapes. This enabled them to have exclusive shapes and to remove the mold, as it was their property, to another factory to fill orders if needed. This practice of "private mold work" was common in mid-century American glass and the use of it by Lotus fits industry common practices.

Francis D. Hanse; Ralph Wilson, etching plate maker for Lotus; John Morgan, head etcher; and W.L. Groves, head cutter, at Lotus, inspecting ware. 1940s. Photo by Barnesville Enterprise.

Francis (F.D.) Hanse and Matthew (M.A.) Hanse, father and son, at a trade show, probably Chicago, proudly display a decorated, slumped tray. Circa 1950s. Photo by Adams & Frank, Chicago. Hanse family collection.

Across the U.S. Lotus was featured in the best markets. From Macy's and Marshall-Fields to Lazarus and fine jewelry stores, Lotus could be found. In an interview with a newspaper at the time of closing, it was stated that "many older Lotus designs were based on, or made to match, Syracuse china patterns." A perfectly good explanation, as Lotus glass was often marketed in jewelry and fine stores selling china and crystal to brides and homemakers. Don Hanse reported in 1996 that, "we did an extensive amount of work for the State Department. We did table service for them." The wares were used for formal occasions in US Embassies around the globe and in the US. The single largest order ever produced by Lotus is reported by Hanse as the thousands of stems for the opening of the Ritz Carlton in Chicago.

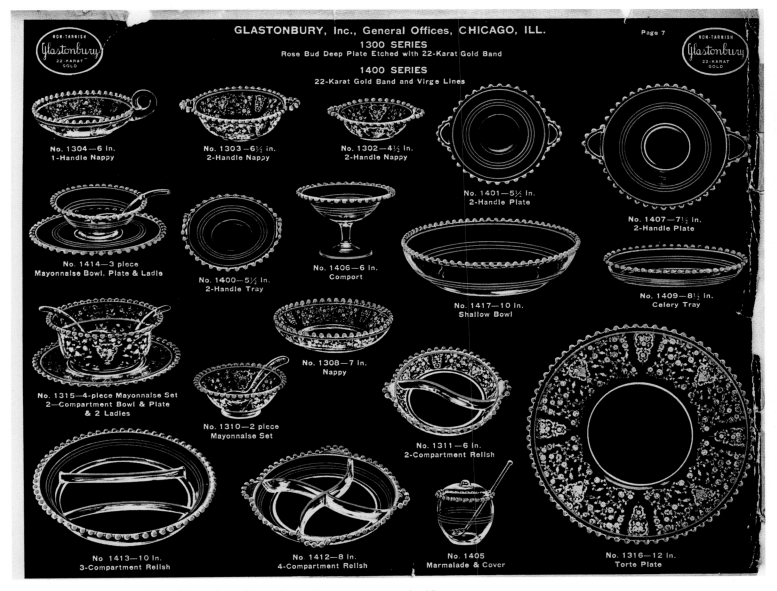

A circa 1950s catalog page from Glastonbury, Inc., a decorating company acquired by Lotus in 1960. The page shows Imperial glass candlewick shapes plate etched and gold gilded, both processes also utilized by Lotus. Several Glastonbury decorations and patterns were continued by Lotus after the acquisition. Replacements, LTD. collection.

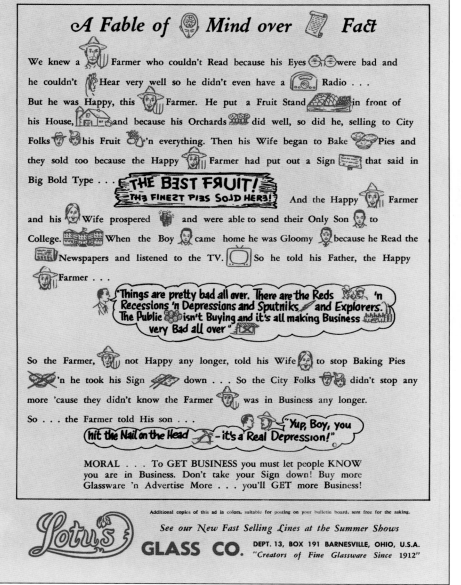

This wildly humorous ad from Lotus is circa 1957 due to the references to Sputnik, the USSR satellite that so fascinated the world. Source and date unknown. Hanse family collection.

Circa 1950, silkscreen work was added to the decorating techniques employed at Lotus. Silk screened tumblers and slumped flat glass became popular products in the next several decades.

Using hand applied luster, a paint-like coloring that is fired at high temperatures to affix it permanently to the glass, Lotus created these very 1950s-looking colored wares. The Catalina line was surely "up to date." Undated ad.

Lotus silk screening was not accomplished by a common industry standard of hot processes, but a cold process that required each piece be done by hand. This slower process allowed for closer registry of multiple colors and a more detailed, exact finished product.

Lotus acquired The Glastonbury Co., a Chicago based glass decorator, in 1960. Some of the Glastonbury patterns were continued as production by Lotus. However, the Glastonbury part of the Lotus story is a small footnote within a much larger story.

By 1995 trends toward casual dining and world imports both had taken their tolls on the markets served by Lotus. Their number of employees had dwindled to twelve people. A number of Barnesville families worked, like the Hanse family, for decades and even generations at Lotus Glass. Their contribution and skills should be remembered as well.

Don Hanse, grandson of M.A., began working at Lotus in 1965 and became president after the death of his father, Francis. Rick Hanse, another grandson, joined his brother in the mid-1970s in managing the company business and became vice president and oversaw the silk screening department. The company ceased operation December 31, 1995 and the physical assets were dispersed at auction. After eighty-three years of production, nine employees remained immediately before the closing in 1995.

Ever the experimenters, Lotus slumped or bent this textured flat glass by using heat and then added color enamels to the back side in their Cathedral line of serving pieces. Looking back it seems amazingly 1950-60s-ish. Undated ad.

# Cathedral *Bent Glass*

## by *Lotus*

An early American reproduction with a figured prism effect. Now in four colors . . . . Emerald Green, Victoria Blue, Amethyst and True Amber . . . that add beauty to modern living.

| | |
|---|---|
| A—12" Circle Cake Plate | $ 2.50 |
| B—7 x 18", 3 Section Divided | 2.50 |
| C—4" Square Coaster or Ash Tray | .60 |
| D—6 x 18", Rectangle Hor d'oevure | 2.50 |
| E—8" Square Cake or Salad | 1.50 |
| F—3 x 6" Oblong Ash Tray or Mint | .60 |
| G—5" Circle Mint or Canape | 1.25 |
| H—5½" Square Mint or Canape | 1.20 |
| I—10 x 16" Rectangle Sandwich Tray | 2.50 |
| J—8" Circle .Cake or Salad | 1.75 |
| K—8 x 14", 3-Section Divided | 2.00 |
| L—12" Square Cake Plate | 2.00 |
| *—14" Square Cake Plate | 2.50 |
| *—8 x 14" Rectangle Canape Tray | 2.00 |
| *—14" Circle Cake Plate | 3.00 |

* Not Illustrated.

BE SURE TO SPECIFY COLOR WHEN ORDERING

*Creators of Fine Glass Since 1912*

If you are not listed in Dun & Bradstreet, please enclose check for the full amount of the order. All orders under $25 will carry 15% handling charge.

THE *Lotus* GLASS CO.

DEPT. 11    BOX 191
BARNESVILLE, OHIO, U.S.A.

## "TINKLING" BELLS

*Brocade*

*Serenity*

*Virginia*

An old favorite in a new dress. Lotus full lead ringing crystal bells are now available in the latest popular stemware patterns. All gold encrustations are 22 karat pure gold applied by the exclusive Lotus process. American Crystal bells that really ring and they're positively irresistible. Individually gift boxed.

*Georgian*

*Lotus*

THE LOTUS GLASS COMPANY, Inc.
BARNESVILLE, OHIO  U.S.A.  43713

Lotus continued to focus on decorating glass, but novelty bells were being promoted in this 1966 *China, Glass & Lamps* ad of August that year.

# Whose Glass Blanks Are These Anyway?

A listing of the glass manufacturers whose glass is recognized in this book and those reported to me by the Hanse family as their suppliers include:

Anchor Hocking Glass, Lancaster, Ohio
Bryce of Mt. Pleasant, Pennsylvania
Cambridge of Cambridge, Ohio
Central Glass of Wheeling, West Virginia
Duncan & Miller of Washington, Pennsylvania
Fostoria of Moundsville, West Virginia
Heisey of Newark, Ohio
Imperial Glass, Bellaire, Ohio
Judel Glass of Salem, West Virginia
Lancaster Glass of Lancaster, Ohio
Libbey Glass of Toledo, Ohio
Louie Glass of Weston, West Virginia
Mid-Atlantic Glass of Ellenboro, West Virginia
Morgantown Glassware Guild, Morgantown, West Virginia
New Martinsville Glass of New Martinsville, West Virginia
Paden City Glass of Paden City, West Virginia
Weston Glass of Weston, West Virginia
Viking Glass, New Martinsville, West Virginia

*Opposite Page:*
The use of acid to etch the glass, then 22 karat was gold hand painted on and the object was fired. This was perhaps the most successful technique used over many decades by Lotus. This handmade, hand decorated punch bowl dates from 1960-70s and is indeed stylish and classy.

Georgian #889
with #889 Encrusted cups
22 Karat Paste Gold

#250—14 pc. Punch Set
with glass ladle
THE Lotus GLASS CO.
Barnesville, Ohio

The aerial view of the factory, from near the end of time, shows the expansion and growth since the Barnesville, Ohio, building was erected in 1915. Hanse family collection.

# Chapter Two
# How to Use This Book

The greatest thing about this book is that it relies only on original Lotus source materials to attribute the glass. There can be no doubt about attribution, names or numbers when all of the images used are actually those from the original manufacturer. The opportunity for a historian to access such a trove of primary source material is rare. The quality of images in this work is inconsistent, being limited by the type and condition of each image selected for use. Decisions were made and images included based on the importance of what they tell. At times, the quality is far less than ideal but the end result is a broad based, visually wonderful example of Lotus ware spanning parts of eight decades.

I have used books where I am compelled to leaf through the pages, looking for, hoping to find, the object I seek. As one who crafts books on collectibles, I dream of ways to make a book easier to use, "user friendly" as my generation has dubbed it. At times, the complexity of the product makes glass books very difficult to organize into easy to use references. With this work on Lotus, I have divided the products only as far as type of decoration. Lotus was a decorating company after all! I regret to admit that, after this initial division, it is a "thumb through the pages" process when looking for your pattern or object.

Within each section, the numbered decorations are shown numerically. Some of the original Lotus information appears with mixed patterns on the sheet or page and those appear in this text arranged by the first decoration appearing on the page. In such events, I have also indexed those other patterns on that page or within the illustration to ensure they are able to be located.

The divisions into sections based on type of decorating work create this book's chapters. Chapter One was a short history, followed by this section on how the book is organized, then Chapter Three begins with the original Lotus product line of cut glass. The product part of the book shall begin as Lotus began. Much of the Lotus Cut Glass was wheel cut and left gray. That is to say the many of the Lotus cuts are not polished to give a shinny, slicker finish but left with the gray and rough surfaces imparted by the fast turning cutting wheels. This style was popular from roughly World War I through the 1950s and is still used today (in the early 2000s) with such popular lines as Princess House. It requires considerable skill as an artisan. Lotus did more elaborate cutting as some of the vases shown give ample testimony to. Later Lotus cuttings included stemware made to compliment china dinner services and often bearing the same name as the china, just in case a prospective buyer missed the obvious coupling of design. To call gray cutting "etchings" is a terrible misuse of glass history and terminology. To etch a glass is many things, but it is not this style of unpolished cutting.

Next come the plate etched patterns. Chapter Four are those with "No Gold" and Chapter Five includes the "Etched with Gold" lines. The process might be called simply Etched as it is, at its simplest, the use of acid to etch the glass. Plate etchings are created using a metal plate into which the pattern is cut. Production of plate etched glass begins when the pattern is lifted from the metal plate by first covering the plate with hot wax, then a thin paper is laid on the wax covered metal plate and hand rubbed, which lifts the wax from the plate to the paper. This results in the deeper, cut pattern of the plate now appearing in the un-waxed areas on the paper. The paper is wrapped around the glass to be decorated and again it is rubbed, this time transferring the wax on to the surface of the glass.

The original design from the plate now appears as the exposed bare glass outlined in the wax. Dipping the wax-coated glass into an acid solution allows the exposed, un-waxed portions of the glass to be eaten away by the acid.

The result after the acid bath is that the un-waxed areas of the pattern have been "etched" by the exposure to the acid and now appear on the glass surface as the same design originally carved into the metal plate while the remainder of the object has been protected by the wax. A rinse bath removes the wax and lingering acid, with the final product showing the pattern, as carved in to the metal plate, now as a slightly rough, acid eaten gray pattern on the glass. It is a labor intensive process requiring time and skilled labor. The passage of time has made it popular with collectors, but it requires far less of an artisan than hand cutting.

As previously stated, the chapters in this book are etched "No Gold" and followed by the etched with gold decoration. The appearance of any gold as banding, encrustation (layering gold over the etched pattern) or other gold application would place the objects and pattern in this second chapter.

The following chapter, Chapter Six, includes those patterns painted or using enamel as a medium for decoration. Colorful and fun patterns are found here.

Silver Deposit decoration follows in Chapter Seven, a section dedicated to the process of affixing a thin layer of sterling silver to the glass surface. This decorative process was popular in the early decades of the twentieth century and was always expensive. Sterling Silver on black glass created some of the most popular and dramatic glass decorations of the early twentieth century.

Decorated tumblers are in Chapter Eight, where images of silk screened and other decorated tumblers are shown. Lotus and other glass producers and decorators produced decorated tumblers in amazing quantities and varieties in the 1950s and later. The "Dallas" TV series used a Lotus oil theme decorated tumbler, testimony to the enduring popularity of this form. There are no individual captions or value suggestions for this chapter.

The final product chapter on miscellany catches an additional sampling of the many diverse decorations that do not necessarily fit well elsewhere. These images do not bear individual captions or value suggestions.

It is imperative that readers and students of glass realize that this work encompasses only a small percentage of the scope of Lotus Glass production. In selecting images for this book literally several hundred illustrations from literature were edited out of the final book. Some images not included were similar to those used, some were of poor quality, some were later in time. My decision was made to focus on earlier production with a light hand on the later twentieth century wares, but to be certain to include later production as a teaser for future writing and research by others.

What began as a grand idea became complex and burdening. One of the fun goals of this project at the outset was to identify the glass blanks used by Lotus. This seemed a simple task. The idea was to identify the source of the glass blank where I could. And I have done so. After a fashion. With the help of several people, we have made attempts to name the known manufacturer of the glass. However, the same blanks are used over and over for various patterns and decorations appearing in this book on different pages. An effort has been made, a significant effort, to name many of the blanks each time they are shown used by Lotus. The manufacturers of some blanks simply are not known, others lack characteristics that would allow attribution. Others do indeed appear on known blanks with known line numbers. The effort to identify blanks is not the same as identifying the blank every time it has been used. The mass of data simply became overwhelming. There are notes on many pages giving source information for the manufacturer of the glass. The notes about the blanks are not extensively cross identified. Pattern names and numbers are well represented in the Index. Please browse other patterns to seek additional information on the source of the same shaped blank.

Enjoy the book, it has been an enjoyable project to create.

# Pricing

Pricing information: please read this carefully and take heed. For most of us who craft books on glass, the most difficult part is suggesting value. Books without price guides do not market well. Thus, I offer suggested price ranges. Note that for most of the products shown in this book, there is no body of sales data from which to establish pricing guidelines. I offer suggestions based on similar pattern prices, on the form or color as potentially desirable, and on my experience in dealing in glass since 1971. I did consult with dealer friends, sending them photocopies of the illustrations and asking that they tell me their suggested pricing. I used this—at times agreeing, at times being amazed by others suggestions. In the end, I made the best decisions I could. However, the price suggestion rendered in this book are only that—suggestions. Do not base your decision as an investment or assurance of resale on the figures I provide. What appears here are only one author's suggestions of what the illustrated item *MIGHT* be worth on the retail market. Suggestions are neither offers to buy nor assurances of a selling price. Suggestions are only that. Please use them accordingly and as intended to guide your own judgment.

# Chapter Three
# Cut Patterns

Cutting No. 2
All crystal. Pre-1930 Lotus catalog.
Whiskey, $2-5; 8 oz. tumbler, $2-4; ice tea, 10 oz., $3-6; iced tea, 12 oz., $2-4; handled iced tea, $6-10; wine, $2-6; sherbet, $2-6; goblet, 9 oz., $6-12; sugar, $8-12; creamer, $8-12; bowl/ mayo, plate and ladle, $10-16; sherbet, low, $2-5; guest room set, $18-26; syrup, 12 oz., $8-12; syrup, 7 oz., $6-10; jam jar with cover, $10-16; footed berry/compote, $8-18; covered iced tea jug, $22-36; pint ice tea with lid, $18- 32; table tumbler, $2-6; 3 pint jug, $16-28.

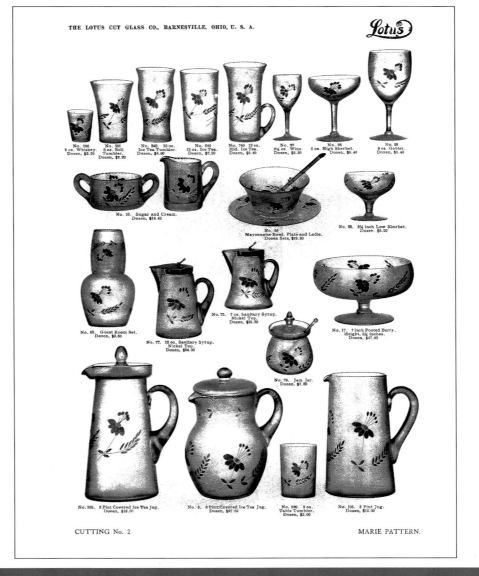

THE LOTUS CUT GLASS CO., BARNESVILLE, OHIO, U. S. A.

CUTTING No. 2

MARIE PATTERN.

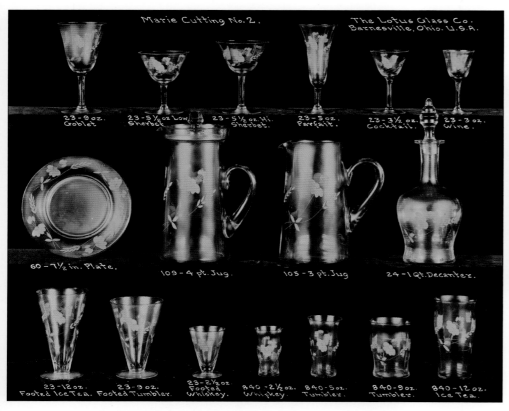

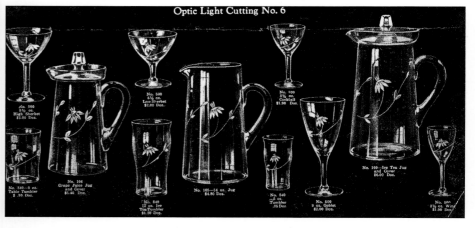

Cutting No. 6
All crystal with an Optic (light vertical ribbing), Lotus original catalog sheet, circa 1920.
High sherbet, $4-6; low sherbet, $2-5; cocktail, $2-5; table tumbler, $2-5; grape juice jug with cover, $18-32; tea tumbler, $4-8; 54 oz. jug, $12-20; tumbler, 5 oz., $2-4; goblet, 9 oz., $8-14; ice tea jug with cover, $20-34; wine, 2 1/2 oz., $4-6.

Cutting No. 2 MARRIE Cut Pattern
Pink/rose and green. Lotus catalog page, pre-1924. Little difference exists between pink and green prices, priced as illustrated.
Goblet, 9 oz., $10-18; sherbet, low, $4-10; sherbet, "hi", $5-12; parfait, $8-16; cocktail, 3 1/2 oz., $4-10; wine, 3 oz., $4-10; plate, $12-18; 4 pint jug with cover, $36-48; 3 pint jug, $24-38; 1 qt. decanter, $32-46; footed iced tea, $6-10; footed tumbler, $5-8; footed whiskey, $4-8; whiskey, $3-6; tumbler, 5 oz., $3-6; tumbler, 9 oz., $4-8, iced tea, $4-10.

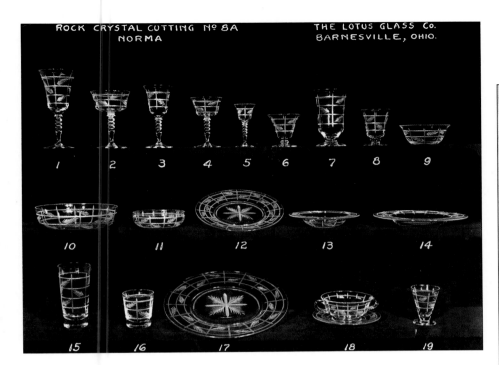

ROCK CRYSTAL CUTTING Nº 8A
NORMA

THE LOTUS GLASS CO.
BARNESVILLE, OHIO.

**Cutting No. 8A NORMA PATTERN**
All crystal "Rock Crystal Cutting." Lotus linen backed photo, circa 1940s.
Goblet (1), $14-20; sherbet (2), $10-18; wine (3), $ 12-18; cocktail (4), $8-14; cordial (5), $14-22; oyster cocktail (6), $8-12; ice tea (7), $10-16; low cocktail (8), $8-12; fruit/dessert bowl (9), $8-12; serving bowl (10), $16-22; nappy (11), $12-16; bread and butter plate or dessert (12), $12-18; salad bowl (13), $10-14; soup bowl (14), $12-20; tumbler (15), $6-10; whiskey (16), $6-12; luncheon plate (17), $14-20; cream soup and under plate (18) set, $ 14-20; footed tumbler (19), $8-12.

**Cutting No. 9**
Rose/pink or amber as noted. Lotus tri-fold flier. After 1924.
Amber pieces would be 50-75% of the price quoted here for pink.
Candlestick #201, each $12-18; bowl, rolled edge console, 10", No. 200, $18-28; cake server/center handled tray, 10", No. 200, $16-24; 3 piece mayonnaise set, No. 200, $14-24; cheese and cracker set, two piece, 10", No. 200, $16-28.

Colors—
Rose
Amber

*Featuring*
*Special Sale Items*

Cutting
No. 9

No. 201—3½ Inch
Low Candlestick

No. 200—10 Inch Rolled Edge Bowl

No. 201—3½ Inch
Low Candlestick

No. 200—10 Inch Handled Cake Plate

No. 200—3-Piece Mayonaise Set

No. 200—10 Inch Cheese and Cracker

Cutting No. 10 GENE
PATTERN
Rose/pink and green. Original
Lotus catalog page. After
1924. Priced as shown, no
significant differences for
pink or green.
Lemon tub and lid, 4 1/2",
$16-28; open handled bon-
bon, $10-18; sugar, $8-18;
cream, $8-18; open handled
cheese, 6 1/2", $10-16; open
handled mint, $10-18; open
handled ice tub, $18-32; open
handled mayonnaise, $10-16;
center handled cake tray, $14-
28; cheese and cracker - two
part, $14-26; basket, 4", $24-
38; basket, 5", $28-42; low-
footed comport, $14-20; low
candlestick, $12-16 each;
rolled edge bowl, console, 10",
$18-28; canoe, $22-32; basket,
6", $32-46.

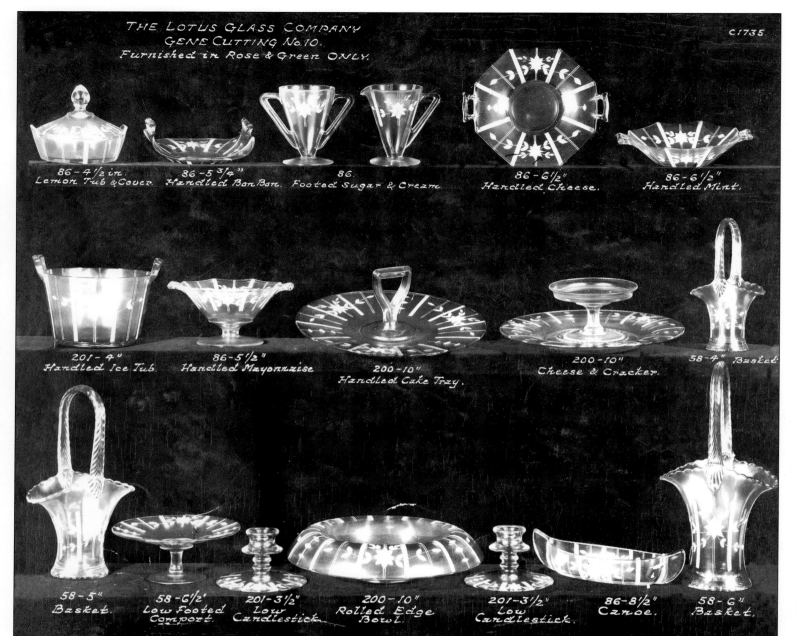

No. 640
12 oz. Ice Tea.
Dozen, $2.50

No. 520
9 oz. Tumbler.
Dozen, $1.70

No. 901
8 oz. Bell Tumbler.
Dozen, $1.80

No. 28
9 oz. Goblet.
Dozen, $5.00

No. 28
3¼ in. High Sherbet.
Dozen, $5.00

No. 28
3¼ in. Low Sherbet.
Dozen, $4.80

No. 105. 3 Pint Jug.
Dozen, $9.60

DISCONTINUED.

CUTTING No. 12

GRAPE PATTERN.

Cutting No. 12 GRAPE PATTERN
Crystal only. Pre-1924 Lotus Cut Glass catalog.
Iced tea, 12 oz., $2-5; Tumbler, 9 oz., $2-4; bell tumbler, 8 oz., $2-6; goblet, 9 oz., $4-6; high sherbet, $2-4; low sherbet, $2-4; 3 pint jug, $14-24; bell jug lemonade, $16-28.
Note: This grape cutting is similar to the cutting produced at dozens of other cut glass shops across the US and beyond. On the jugs it appears more distinguishable.

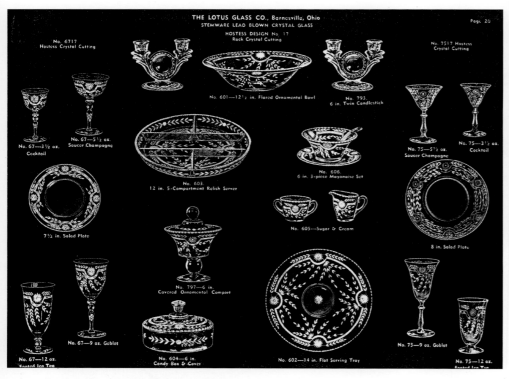

Cutting No. 19
"Topaz or Rose only." Lotus catalog page circa 1930-40s.
Salad bowl, handled, $30-42; mayonnaise set, 3 pieces, $34-48: tall comport,
$36-46; crimped bowl, handled, $30-42; sugar, $18-28; creamer, $18-28; tall
candlestick, $16-28 each; console bowl, $26-38; low comport, $30-38: cheese
and cracker, two pieces, $30-42; candy box with lid, $36-46; handled cake tray/
server, $28-38; handled sandwich tray, $28-38.
The Glass Blanks: All the blanks for this pattern illustrated are on Paden City
Glass in the Crow's Foot line, #412 square shape.

Cutting No. 17 HOSTESS PATTERN
Crystal only. "Rock Crystal" cut pattern. Catalog page circa 1940s.
On the left of the page in the # 6717 line are: cocktail, 3 1/2 oz., $14-18; 5 1/2 oz. saucer
champagne, $16-18; plate, salad, 7 1/2", $14-20; iced tea, footed, 12 oz., $16-20; and goblet,
9 oz., $18-22. The center shows the twin candlesticks, 6", each $22-28; flared ornamental
bowl, 12 1/2", $26-38; relish, 5 part divided, $24-32; mayo/3 piece set, $20-32; comport/
candy with cover, 6", $26-38; cream and sugar, each $12-16; candy box w/ lid, 6", $20-24;
and tray, flat serving, 12", $18-28. On the left in #7517 are the saucer champagne, 5 1/2
oz., $16-20; cocktail, 3 1/2 oz., $14-20; plate, salad, 8", $16-22; goblet, 9 oz., $18-24; and ice
tea, footed, 12 oz., $16-22.
Note: this page features two stem lines utilizing one common line of serving and flat
pieces, excepting the salad plate. On the page left is #6717 stemware and on the right is
#7517 cut stem shapes.
The Glass Blanks: The bowl and candlestick on the top row are Duncan & Miller glass
blanks. The candlesticks are Duncan's Pall Mall #30 blanks. The covered comport/ candy
#797 is Paden City.

THE LOTUS GLASS COMPANY, Barnesville, Ohio, U. S. A.
Rock Crystal Cutting No. 24
"MAJESTY"
Page 18

No. 727—8 in.
Flip Vase

No. 835—2 qt.
Ice Lip Jug

No. 728—12 in.
2-Hid. Oblong Platter

No. 797—6 in.
Tall Covered Compart

No. 495—11 in.
Lily Bowl

No. 936
Sugar & Creamer

No. 794—6 in.
Twin Candlestick

No. 75—12 in.
Console Bowl

No. 794—6 in.
Twin Candlestick

No. 492—14 in.
Flat Plate

No. 71—7 in.
Tall Compart

No. 724—12 in.
Cheese & Cracker

No. 760—3-Piece
Mayonnaise Set

No. 491—10 in.
Salad Bowl

No. 105—11 in.
Footed Vase

No. 796—6 in.

No. 494—12 in.
Flared Bowl

No. 304—12 in.

No. 493—14 in.

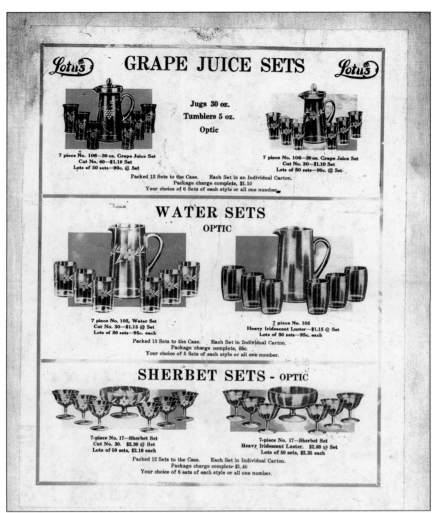

Cutting No. 24 MAJESTY PATTERN
All crystal. Lotus catalog page circa 1940s.
Flip vase, 8", $12-16; jug, ice lip, 2 qt., $24-34; platter, oblong tab handled, 12", $14-18; comport/candy with lid, 6", $24-28; bowl, lily, 11", $14-18; sugar or creamer, each $9-12; twin candlestick, 6", each $16-22; bowl, console, 12", $24-30; plate, flat torte, 14", $18-24; comport, tall, 7", $12-18; vase, footed, 11", $18-24; cheese and cracker, 12", $16-20; mayonnaise set, 3 piece, $20-26; bowl, salad, 10", $18-24; candy box, footed with lid, $16-22; bowl, flared, 12", $16-22; relish, 5 part divided, 12", $16-22; plate, rolled edge torte, 14", $18-24.
The Glass Blanks: the #797 comport/candy is Paden City Glass, the oblong platter appears to be Fostoria Lafayette #2440 (?), and the console bowl may be Fostoria #2375.

Cutting No. 30 and other Cuttings.
All Crystal. Lotus sheet/promotional flier. Circa 1920s.
Grape juice set, seven pieces plus lid, cut No. 40, $30-45 set; grape juice set seven pieces plus lid, cut No. 30, $30-45 set. Water set, seven pieces, cut No. 30, $30-45 set; heavy Iridescent 7 piece set, $25-35 set; sherbet set, seven pieces, cut No. 30, $18-34 set; heavy iridescent 7 piece set, $16-32 set.

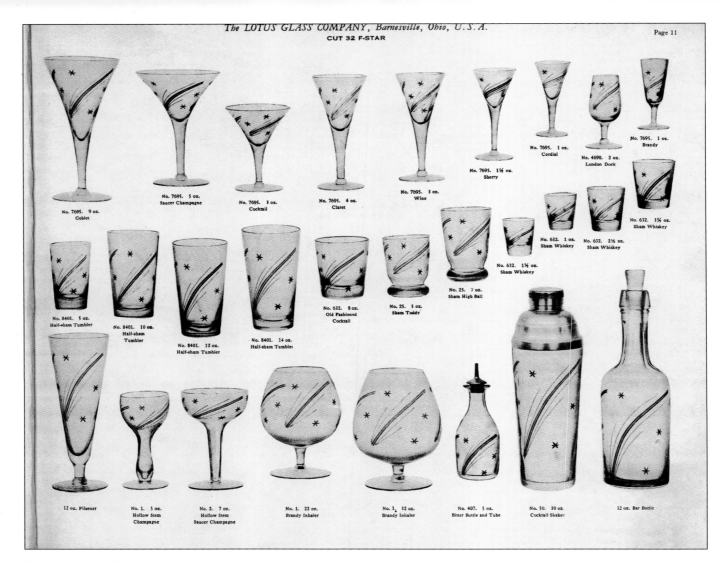

No. 7695. 9 oz. Goblet

No. 7695. 5 oz. Saucer Champagne

No. 7695. 3 oz. Cocktail

No. 7695. 4 oz. Claret

No. 7695. 3 oz. Wine

No. 7695. 1½ oz. Sherry

No. 7695. 1 oz. Cordial

No. 4690. 2 oz. London Dock

No. 7695. 1 oz. Brandy

No. 632. 1 oz. Sham Whiskey

No. 632. 2½ oz. Sham Whiskey

No. 632. 3½ oz. Sham Whiskey

No. 632. 1½ oz. Sham Whiskey

No. 8401. 5 oz. Half-sham Tumbler

No. 8401. 10 oz. Half-sham Tumbler

No. 8401. 12 oz. Half-sham Tumbler

No. 8401. 14 oz. Half-sham Tumbler

No. 632. 8 oz. Old Fashioned Cocktail

No. 25. 5 oz. Sham Toddy

No. 25. 7 oz. Sham High Ball

12 oz. Pilsener

No. 1. 5 oz. Hollow Stem Champagne

No. 2. 7 oz. Hollow Stem Saucer Champagne

No. 1. 22 oz. Brandy Inhaler

No. 1. 32 oz. Brandy Inhaler

No. 407. 5 oz. Bitter Bottle and Tube

No. 50. 30 oz. Cocktail Shaker

32 oz. Bar Bottle

Cutting No 32-F STAR pattern.
All Crystal. Lotus catalog circa 1937-38.
Goblet, 9 oz., $12-18; saucer champagne, $10-14; cocktail, $10-12; claret, $10-12; wine, $10-12; sherry, $14-18; cordial, $14-18; London Dock, $8-12; brandy, $10-14; half sham tumbler, 5 oz., $4-8; half sham tumbler, 10 oz., $4-8; half sham tumbler, 12 oz., $5-10; half sham tumbler, 14 oz., $6-12; old fashioned, 8 oz., $6-10; sham toddy, 5 oz., $4-8; sham high ball, 7 oz., $5-10; sham whiskey, 1 1/2 oz., $4-8; sham whiskey, 1 oz., $4-8; sham whiskey, 2 1/2 oz., $4-8; sham whiskey, 3 1/2 oz., $4-8; pilsner, 12 oz., $8-14; hollow stem champagne, 5 oz., $10-14; hollow stem champagne, 7 oz., $14-18; brandy inhaler, 22 oz., $10-16; brandy inhaler, 32 oz., $12-18; bitter bottle and tube, $14-20; cocktail shaker with chrome lid, $30-45; bar bottle and glass stopper, $20-36.
Note: The use of the word "sham" in language today is related to this form of tumbler where extra glass was created at the bottom to add weight and height to a drinking vessel, giving the illusion of getting more than was there. It remains an active word in glass bar ware.

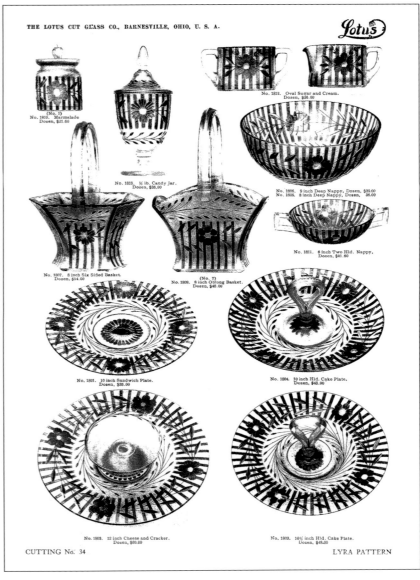

Cutting No. 34 LYRA PATTERN
All crystal. Lotus catalog pre-1924.
Plate, 6", $4-6; bowl/deep nappy, $6-8; covered syrup, $18-24; corset form vase, $14-22; covered candy box, 6", $14-18; covered candy box, 8", $18-24; bowl/two handled nappy, $14-16; full sham tumbler, $8-12; 3 pint tankard jug, $24-30; 3 pint squat jug, $24-30; 4 pint jug, bell, $26-36.
The Glass Blanks: The two handled nappy (bowl) is Heisey Glass Yeoman #1186, the squat jug is Heisey #4163, and the tankard jug is Heisey.

Cutting No. 34 LYRA PATTERN
All Crystal. Lotus catalog pre-1924.
Marmalade w/ lid, $14-18; candy jar, footed, $18-26; oval cream, $8-12; oval sugar, $8-12; basket, six sided, 8", $95-125; basket, oblong, 8", $95-125; bowl/ nappy, 8", $12-18; bowl/nappy, 9", $14-18; bowl/nappy, two handled, 6", $10-16; plate, sandwich, 10", $12-16; handled cake plate/server, 10", $10-14; cheese and cracker, two part, 12", $18-22; handled cake plate/server, 10 1/2", $12-14.
The Glass Blanks: The two handled nappy (bowl) is Heisey Glass Yeoman #1186 and the baskets are Heisey Glass.

THE LOTUS CUT GLASS CO. CUTTING NO. 37.
BARNESVILLE, OHIO.

NO. 28. CORDIAL.  NO. 28. SHERRY.  NO. 29. SHERRY.  NO. 28. WINE.  NO. 28. CLARET.  NO. 28. 5 OZ. CHAMP.  NO. 28. GOBLET.

NO. 28. RHINE WINE.  NO. 28. SAU. CHAMP.  NO. 28. COCKTAIL.  NO. 28. EGG.  NO. 28-3½" SHERBET.  NO. 28. IND. ALMOND.

NO. 28. CUSTARD.  NO. 28. LARGE ALMOND.  NO. 17. 7" BERRY.  NO. 36-6" CONFECTION.

Cutting No. 37
All Crystal. Lotus linen backed catalog photo pre-1924.
Cordial, $8-14; sherry, flared, $5-8; sherry, cupped, $5-8; wine, $5-8; claret, $7-9;
champagne, 5 oz., $7-9; goblet, $8-10; Rhine wine, $5-8; saucer champagne, $4-6;
cocktail, $4-6; egg cup, $6-8; sherbet, $4-6; individual almond, $5-8; custard/punch cup,
$4-6; almond, large, $4-6; berry compote, $8-12; confection/tall compote, $12-14.

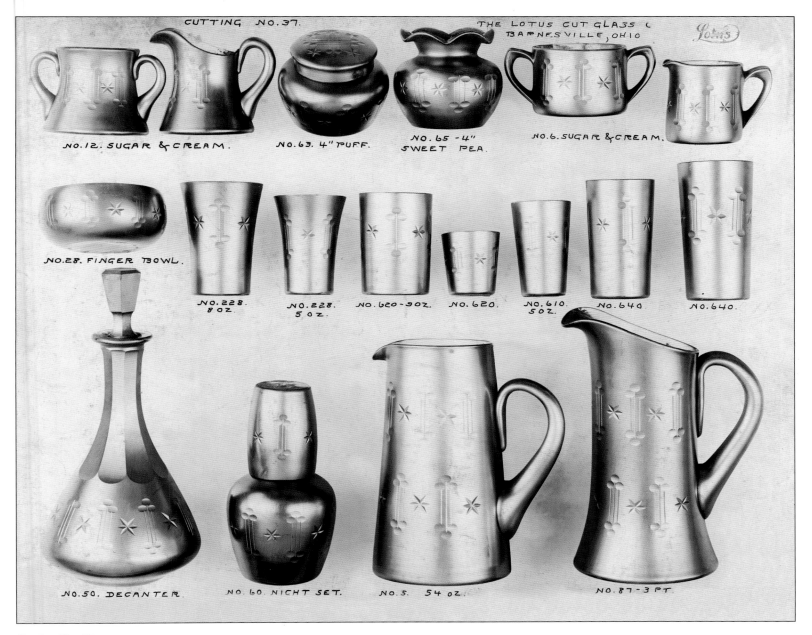

Cutting No. 37
All Crystal. Lotus Cut Glass Co. catalog page pre-1924.
Sugar, bell, $10-14; creamer, bell, $10-14; puff, 4" box w/ lid, $20-32; sweet pea vase, $10-14; sugar, straight-sided, $8-10; creamer, straight-sided, $8-10; finger bowl, $4-6; tumbler, 8 oz., $4-6; tumbler, soda, 5 oz., $4-6; tumbler, table, 9 oz., $4-6; whiskey, $4-6; tumbler, 5 oz., $2-4; tumbler, $4-6; tumbler, tall, $6-8; decanter with stopper, $20-32; night set w/ tumbler, $24-36; jug, tankard, 54 oz., $24-32; jug, 3 pint, belled, $26-38.

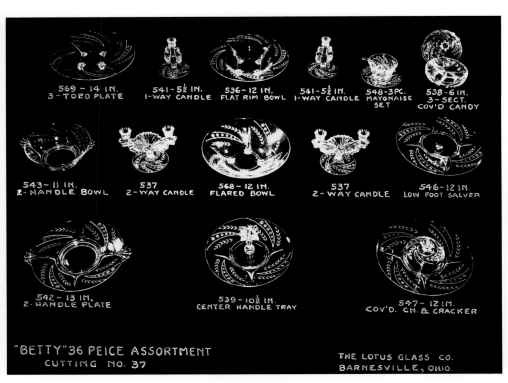

Cutting No. 37 (the newer version) BETTY PATTERN
Appears Crystal. Loose Lotus black and white linen backed photo circa 1930-40s.
Plate, three-toed (see 4 toes?-ed.) 14", $14-20; candle stick, 5 1/2", each $12-18; bowl, flat rim, 12", $14-20; mayonnaise set, 3 piece, $18-26; candy dish, 3 part divided with lid, $22-30; bowl, two handled, 11", $14-20; candle, 2 light, each $28-36; bowl, flared/console, $14-20; cake salver, low, 12", $24-34; plate, two handled, 13", $14-18; center handled server/tray, 10 1/2", $18-24; cheese and cracker, two part covered, 12", $20-32.
The Glass Blanks: All the blanks for this pattern illustrated are Paden City Glass line #221 Maya.

Cutting No. 38 VINE LINE PATTERN
All crystal. Lotus Cut Glass Co. catalog page, pre-1924.
Goblet, $6-10; ice tea, handled, $8-12; tumbler, tea, $4-6; tumbler, bell, $3-5; tumbler, table, 7 oz., $3-5; tumbler, table, 9 oz., $3-5; horseradish set, two part, $30-38; guest room set/tumbler, $36-46; sherbet, low, $3-5; sherbet, high, $3-5; syrup with metal lid, $14-18; sugar, $8-10; creamer, $8-10; bud vase, 10", $8-10; candy jar with lid, $18-24; berry compote, 7", $12-22; jug, refrigerator, 3 pint, $24-34; jug, 4 pint, belled, $38-44; jug, ice tea with lid, 3 pint, $45-55.

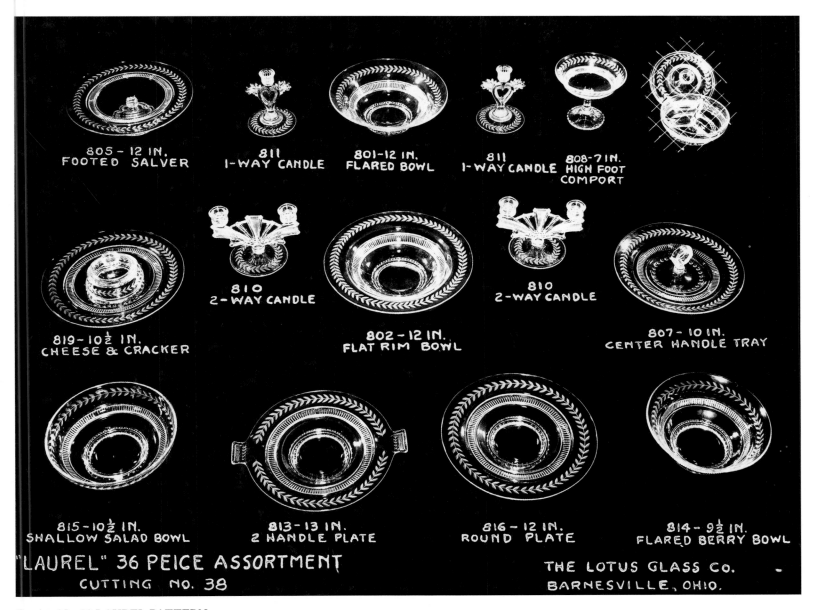

805 – 12 IN.
FOOTED SALVER

811
1-WAY CANDLE

801-12 IN.
FLARED BOWL

811
1-WAY CANDLE

808-7 IN.
HIGH FOOT
COMPORT

810
2-WAY CANDLE

802 – 12 IN.
FLAT RIM BOWL

810
2-WAY CANDLE

819-10½ IN.
CHEESE & CRACKER

807 – 10 IN.
CENTER HANDLE TRAY

815-10½ IN.
SHALLOW SALAD BOWL

813-13 IN.
2 HANDLE PLATE

816 – 12 IN.
ROUND PLATE

814 – 9½ IN.
FLARED BERRY BOWL

"LAUREL" 36 PEICE ASSORTMENT
CUTTING NO. 38

THE LOTUS GLASS CO.
BARNESVILLE, OHIO.

Cutting No. 38 LAUREL PATTERN.
Appears crystal. Lotus black and white linen backed photo catalog page circa 1940s.
Salver, cake, footed, 12", $18-26; candle stick, single light, $30-38; flared bowl/console,
12", $24-34; comport, high, 7", $14-20; candy, 3 part divided w/lid, $20-28; cheese and
cracker, two piece, 10 1/2", $26-32; candle, 2 light, each $20-32; bowl, flat rim, 12", $20-34;
tray, center handled/cake, 10", $16-24; bowl, shallow salad, 10 1/2", $14-18; plate, two tab
handled, 13", $12-16; plate, torte, 12", $14-18; bowl, berry, flared, 9 1/2", $14-18.
The Glass Blanks: These are all Paden City line #330 Cavendish blanks.

Cutting No. 40
All crystal. Lotus Cut Glass black and white linen backed photo catalog page pre-1924.
Custard/punch cup, $2-5; finger bowl, $3-5; puff box, 4" with lid, $28-36; sugar, $4-8;
creamer, $4-8; whiskey, $4-6; tumbler, 5 oz., $2-4; tumbler, $3-5; tumbler, tall, $4-6;
tumbler, table, 9 oz., $3-5; tumbler, soda, 8 oz., $2-4; plate, $5-8; bowl/nappy, 6", $3-5;
sweet pea vase, 4", $12-14; vase, footed, 6", $14-16; vase, bulbous, flared, 6", $8-10; night
set w/ tumbler, $24-36; jug, 3 pint squat, $24-38; jug, 3 pint bell, $22-28; jug, tankard,
$24-32.

No. 558—11 in.
Center Hld. Sandwich

No. 557—11 in.
2-Hld. Salad Bowl

No. 552—7 in.
3-part Candy and Cover

No. 551—5 in.
Candle

No. 550—12 in.
Flat Rim Bowl

No. 551—5 in.
Candle

No. 560—11½ in.
Low Footed Salver

No. 555—6 in.
2-Way Candlestick

No. 554—12½ in.
Flared Console Bowl

No. 555—6 in.
2-Way Candlestick

No. 562
3-pc. Mayonnaise Set

No. 559—10 in.
Footed Comport

No. 561—10½ in.
Cheese and Cracker

No. 556—13 in.
Hld. Sandwich Plate

Cutting No. 40 (the newer version) JANE PATTERN
All crystal. Lotus catalog circa 1937-38. Gray cutting.
Sandwich tray, center handled, 11", $16-24; bowl, salad, 2 handled, 11", $14-18;
candy, 3 part divided with lid, $18-26; candle, single light, 5", each $12-18; bowl,
flat rim/console, 12", $12-18; salver, cake, low-footed, 11 1/2", $22-32; candle, two
light, 6", each $18-28; bowl, flared console, 12 1/2", $14-22; mayonnaise set, 3
part, $18-24; comport, footed, 10", $14-20; cheese and cracker, two part, 10 1/2",
$18-24; plate, sandwich, two handled, 13", $14-18.
The Glass Blanks: All Paden City Glass line #220 Largo.

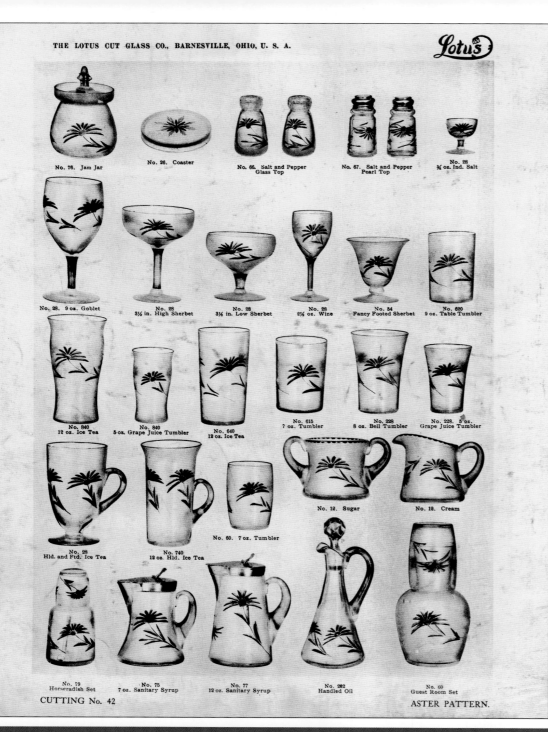

THE LOTUS CUT GLASS CO., BARNESVILLE, OHIO, U. S. A.

*Lotus*

No. 76. Jam Jar     No. 26. Coaster     No. 65. Salt and Pepper Glass Top     No. 67. Salt and Pepper Pearl Top     No. 28 ¾ oz. Ind. Salt

No. 28. 9 oz. Goblet    No. 28 3½ in. High Sherbet    No. 28 3½ in. Low Sherbet    No. 28 2½ oz. Wine    No. 54 Fancy Footed Sherbet    No. 620 9 oz. Table Tumbler

No. 840 12 oz. Ice Tea    No. 840 5-oz. Grape Juice Tumbler    No. 640 12 oz. Ice Tea    No. 615 7 oz. Tumbler    No. 228 8 oz. Bell Tumbler    No. 228. 5 oz. Grape Juice Tumbler

No. 28 Hld. and Ftd. Ice Tea    No. 740 12 oz. Hld. Ice Tea    No. 60. 7 oz. Tumbler    No. 12. Sugar    No. 12. Cream

No. 79 Horseradish Set    No. 75 7 oz. Sanitary Syrup    No. 77 12 oz. Sanitary Syrup    No. 292 Handled Oil    No. 60 Guest Room Set

CUTTING No. 42            ASTER PATTERN.

Cutting No. 42 appeared in an illustrated ad for The Lotus Cut Glass Company in June of 1922 showing the covered jug as a part of an iced tea set. This magazine, *The Keystone*, was a wholesale magazine for jewelers and upper end stores. Note the cost of, $2.75 for each set in 1922! This was not inexpensive even in 1922!

Cutting No. 42 ASTER PATTERN

All Crystal. Lotus Cut Glass black and white catalog page pre-1924. Jam jar w/ lid, $12-18; coaster, $2-4; salt and pepper, glass top, $6-8; salt and pepper, pearl top, $6-8; salt, individual, $8-12; goblet, $8-12; sherbet/saucer champagne, high, $2-5; sherbet, low, $2-5; wine, 2 1/2 oz., $4-6; sherbet, fancy-footed, $2-5; tumbler, table, 9 oz., $2-5; iced tea, 12 oz., $4-6; grape juice, 5 oz., $2-4; iced tea, straight-sided, 12 oz., $4-6; tumbler, table, 7 oz., $2-5; tumbler, bell, 8 oz., $2-5; tumbler, grape juice, bell, 5 oz., $2-5; ice tea, handled and-footed, $6-10; ice tea, handled, 12 oz., $6-10; tumbler, barrel, 7 oz., $2-5; sugar, $8-10; creamer, $8-10; horseradish set, two part, $30-38; syrup w/ metal lid, 7 oz., $16-22; syrup w/ metal lid, 12 oz., $18-22; handled oil with stopper, $18-26; guest room set with tumbler, $28-36.

## Cutting No. 42 ASTER PATTERN

All Crystal. Lotus Cut Glass Co. catalog pre-1924.
Confection compote, 6", $8-14; sandwich plate, center handled, 10", $12-16; cheese and cracker, two part (not shown), $14-16; berry compote, $6-10; jug, grape juice, bulbous base, 18-28; jug, 3 pint, barrel, $14-20; jug, ice tea with lid, 3 pint, $28-38; jug, grape juice, 29 oz., $14-20; jug, 3 pint squat, $14-20; jug, bell, 4 pint, $20-32.

## Cutting No. 45 GOTHIC PATTERN

All Crystal. Lotus Cut Glass Co. catalog pre-1924.
Sherbet, low, $3-5; sherbet, high, $3-5; comport, footed, 6", $8-12; comport, footed, 9" (not shown), $10-16; bowl, 8", $8-10; bowl, 9" (not shown), $10-12; bowl/nappy, 7 1/2" (not shown), $6-10; candy, footed with lid, 10", $18-24; plate, 8 1/2", $7-9; plate, 7 1/2" (not shown), $5-7; plate, 6" (not shown), $3-5; basket, 7 1/2", $28-34; basket, 10" (not shown), $36-42; basket, 12" (not shown), $48-54; tumbler, table, 9 oz., $5-8; jug, 1/2 gallon, $28-36.

CUTTING No. 49

FLORENCE PATTERN.

ALL LEAD GLASS EXCEPT SUGAR AND CREAM.

THE LOTUS GLASS COMPANY, Barnesville, Ohio, U. S. A.
Rock Crystal Cutting No. 63
"FLORENCE"

Cutting No. 49 FLORENCE pattern.
All Crystal. Lotus catalog pre-1924.
Whiskey, 2 1/2 oz., $5-8; tumbler, 5 oz., $3-5; iced tea, 12 oz., $4-6; ice tea, handled, 12 oz., $10-14; cordial, $5-8; wine, 2 1/2 oz., $3-5; café parfait, 6 oz., $4-6; goblet, 9 oz., $10-14; sherbet, low, $3-5; cocktail, 3 1/2 oz., $3-5; sherbet/saucer champagne, tall, 5 oz., $3-5; comport, 6" diameter, $10-14; bowl, berry, footed, 7" diameter, $10-14; creamer, $6-9; sugar, $6-9; guest set, two piece with tumbler, $24-36; jug, ice tea with lid, $26-38; tumbler, table, 9 oz., $3-5; jug, bell, 4 pint, $20-30.
Note: The pattern name Florence was used again by Lotus for the following Cutting No. 63.

Cutting No. 63 FLORENCE Pattern
All crystal. Lotus catalog page circa 1940s.
Flip vase, 8", $12-16; jug, ice lip, 2 qt., $24-34; platter, oblong tab handled, 12", $14-18; comport/candy with lid, 6", $24-28; bowl, lily, 11", $14-18; sugar or creamer, each $9-12; twin candlestick, 6", each $16-22; bowl, console, 12", $24-30; plate, flat torte, 14", $18-24; comport, tall, 7", $12-18; vase, footed, 11", $18-24; cheese and cracker, 12", $16-20; mayonnaise set, 3 piece, $20-26; bowl, salad, 10", $18-24; candy box, footed with lid, $16-22; bowl, flared, 12", $16-22; relish, 5 part divided, 12", $16-22; plate, rolled edge torte, 14", $18-24.
Note: The pattern name Florence was used previously for the cutting shown immediately before this as Cut 49.
The Glass Blanks: the #797 comport/candy is Paden City Glass.

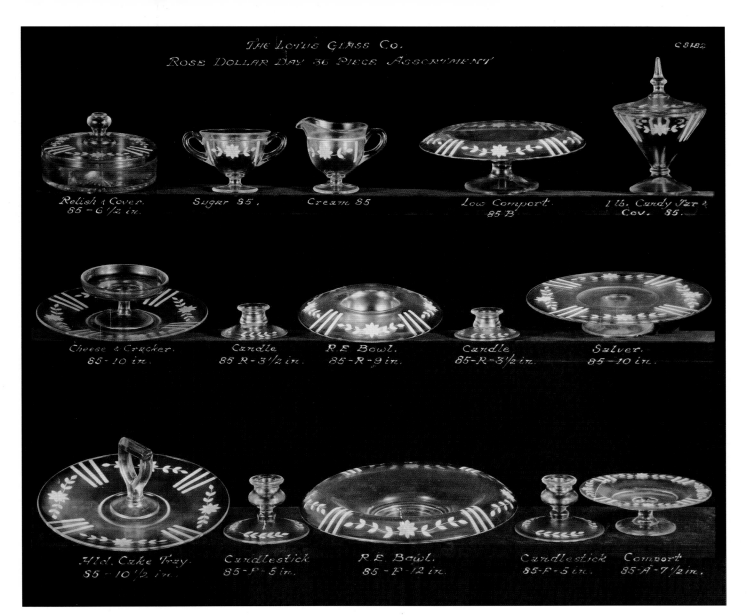

The Lotus Glass Co.
ROSE DOLLAR DAY 36 Piece Assortment

C 8182

Relish & Cover.
85 - 6 1/2 in.

Sugar 85.

Cream 85

Low Comport.
85 B

1 lb. Candy Jar &
Cov. 85.

Cheese & Cracker.
85 - 10 in.

Candle
85 R - 3 1/2 in.

R.E. Bowl.
85 - R - 9 in.

Candle
85 - R - 3 1/2 in.

Salver.
85 - 10 in.

Hld. Cake Tray.
85 - 10 1/2 in.

Candlestick
85 - F - 5 in.

R.E. Bowl.
85 - F - 12 in.

Candlestick
85 - F - 5 in.

Comport
85 - A - 7 1/2 in.

Cutting No. 85
Loose leaf Lotus catalog page, ROSE DOLLAR DAY assortment. All depression era pink.
Catalog page after 1924.
Relish and cover (divided 3 part candy), $20-26; sugar, $10-14; creamer, $10-14; comport, low-footed, rolled rim, $16-22; candy jar, footed with lid, $22-28; cheese and cracker, two part, 10", $16-24; candle, single low, 3 1/2", $10-14; bowl, rolled edge console, 9", $20-32; salver, cake, footed, 10", $28-36; cake tray/center handled server, 10 1/2", $16-20; candlestick, single, 5", each $16-20; bowl, rolled edge, 12" console, $24-36; comport, flat rim, 7 1/2", $18-28.

# The Lotus Cut Glass Co.
## BARNESVILLE,
## OHIO,
## U. S. A.

*Lotus*
TRADE MARK

No. 87—3 Pint Jug
Cut No. 35
No. 87—4 Pint (same shape)

No. 288—8 oz. Tumbler
Cut No. 35

No. 228—8 oz. Tumbler
Cut No. 37

No. 87—3 Pint Jug
Cut No. 37
No. 87—4 Pint (same shape)

MADE IN AMERICA

No. 228—8oz. Tumbler
Cut No. 40

No. 9—3 Pint Jug
Cut No. 40

No. 620—9 oz. Tumbler
Cut No. 42

*(All Cuts one-third size.)*

No. 5—54 oz. Jug
Cut No. 42
No. 3—29 oz. (same shape)

No. 228—8 oz. Tumbler
Cut No. 42

No. 7—Dutch Jug
Cut No. 40

No. 620—9 oz. Tumbler
Cut No. 40

No. 5—54 oz. Jug
Cut No. 40
No. 3—29 oz. (same shape)

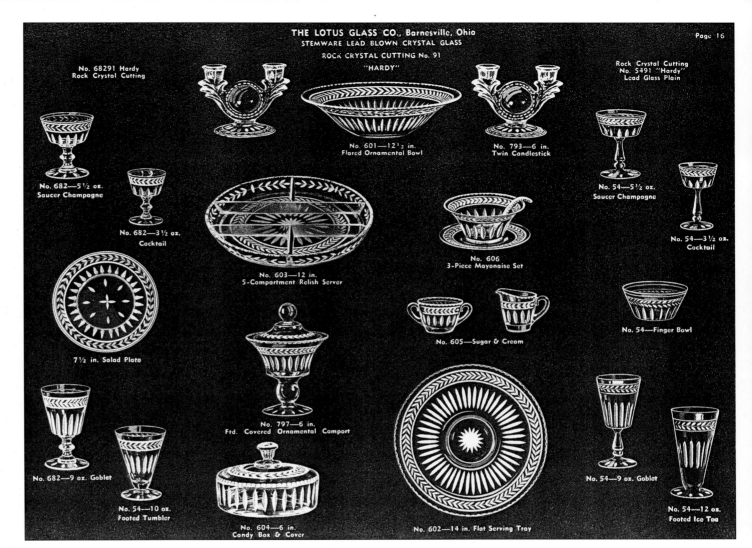

No. 68291 Hardy
Rock Crystal Cutting

Rock Crystal Cutting
No. 5491 "Hardy"
Lead Glass Plain

No. 682—5½ oz.
Saucer Champagne

No. 682—3½ oz.
Cocktail

No. 601—12½ in.
Flared Ornamental Bowl

No. 793—6 in.
Twin Candlestick

No. 54—5½ oz.
Saucer Champagne

No. 54—3½ oz.
Cocktail

No. 603—12 in.
5-Compartment Relish Server

No. 606
3-Piece Mayonaise Set

7½ in. Salad Plate

No. 605—Sugar & Cream

No. 54—Finger Bowl

No. 682—9 oz. Goblet

No. 797—6 in.
Ftd. Covered Ornamental Comport

No. 54—9 oz. Goblet

No. 54—10 oz.
Footed Tumbler

No. 604—6 in.
Candy Box & Cover

No. 602—14 in. Flat Serving Tray

No. 54—12 oz.
Footed Ice Tea

Cutting No. 91 HARDY Pattern
All crystal. Lotus catalog page circa 1940s.
Line 682 and 54 both priced the same: Saucer champagne, $5-8; cocktail, $4-6; goblet, $10-12; iced tea, footed, $10-12; twin candlesticks, 6", each $20-28; bowl, flared, 12 1/2", $14-18; relish, 5 part, $18-24; mayonnaise, 3 part, $18-24; plate, salad, 7 1/2", $8-10; comport/candy with lid, 6", $20-30; sugar or creamer, each $8-10; finger bowl, $6-8; candy box w/ lid, 6", $20-30; tray, flat serving, 14", $22-26.
Note: On the left is Hardy, Cut #91 on stem line 682 and the right is the same cut on stem line 54. Both lines are the same cut and are served by the common flat and serving pieces shown center page.
The Glass Blanks: Most of the forms used on this page appear to be Duncan & Miller. The twin candlestick is Duncan's No. 30. The apparent exception is the "Ftd. Covered Ornamental Comport" which is Paden City.

*Opposite Page:*
Cutting No. 87 and other
All crystal. Lotus single sheet flier pre-1924.
Jug, bell, Cut No. 35, 3 pint, $32-42; 4 pint, $34-44; tumbler, 8 oz., Cut No. 35, $4-6; tumbler, 8 oz., Cut No. 37, $4-6; jug, bell, Cut No. 37, 3 pint, $26-36; 4 pint, $28-38; tumbler, 8 oz., Cut No. 40, $3-5; jug, bell, Cut No. 40, 3 pint, $22-26; tumbler, 9 oz., Cut No. 42, $2-5; jug, tankard, Cut No. 42, 54 oz., $18-28, 29 oz., $16-22; tumbler, 8 oz., Cut No. 42, $2-5; jug, "Dutch", Cut No. 40, $20-24; tumbler, 9 oz., Cut No. 40, $3-5; jug, tankard, Cut No. 40, 54 oz., $26-30; 29 oz., $24-28.

# ROCK CRYSTAL

# EMPRESS

# DESIGN

# No. 671

## THE LOTUS GLASS CO. INC.
### BARNESVILLE, O.

**EMPRESS DESIGN**
**No. 671**

## ROCK CRYSTAL

## EMPRESS DESIGN
## No. 671

*wrong prices*

### Crystal Cut Stem & Base

| No. | | Per doz. |
|---|---|---|
| 671-9 oz. | Goblet | $15.60 |
| 671-5 " | Sau Champ | 15.60 |
| 671-5 " | Low Sherbet | 15.60 |
| 671-5 " | Parfait | 15.60 |
| 671- " | Fruit Salad | 18.00 |
| 671-5 " | Claret | 15.00 |
| 671-3½" | Cocktail | 15.00 |
| 671-¾" | Cordial | 14.40 |
| 671-3 " | Wine | 15.00 |
| 671-12 " | Ftd. Ice Tea | 15.60 |
| 671-9 " | Ftd. Tumbler | 15.60 |
| 671-6 " | Ftd. Tumbler | 15.00 |
| 671-3½" | Ftd. Tumbler | 15.00 |
| 671-8 in. | Salad Plate | 24.00 |
| 671-7½ in | Deep Salad Plate | 20.40 |

### Less Keystone

Cutting No. 671 EMPRESS Pattern.
Crystal. Lotus point of purchase consumer brochure circa 1930s.
Goblet, 9 oz., $12-14; saucer champagne/tall sherbet, $4-6; sherbet, low, $4-6; parfait, 5 oz., $5-8; fruit salad, $5-8; claret, 5 oz., $5-8; cocktail, 3 1/2 oz., $4-6; cordial, 3/4 oz., $12-16; wine, 3 3/4 oz., $4-6; iced tea, footed, $10-14; tumbler, footed, 9 oz., $4-6; tumbler, footed, 6 oz., $3-5; tumbler, footed, 3 1/2 oz., $3-5; plate, salad, 8", $6-10; plate, deep salad/soup bowl, 7 1/2", $6-8.

Cutting No. 701
Rose and green. Lotus three fold brochure. Circa 1920. No significant price differences for either color. As shown: candlestick, single low, 4 3/4", each $16-20; bowl, rolled edge/console, 12", $18-24; covered relish (three part divided candy with lid), $24-28; cheese and cracker, two part, 10", $20-26; whipped cream set/3 part mayonnaise, $24-28; sandwich plate, handled/cake server, 10", $16-22.

Colors
*Rose and Green*

**FEATURING**
## Special Sale Items

Good $ Numbers
For
*Afternoon Teas*
*Euchre—Bridge*
*Favor Parties, Etc.*

## New Octagonal Assortment

## No. 701—36 Piece Octagon Assortment

Single Assortment—One Barrel ............................................. $24.00 per assortment.
Five Barrel Lots or over .................................................... $21.60 per assortment.

### What the assortment consists of and what you get:

| | | | | |
|---|---|---|---|---|
| 6—only No. 701—10 in. Cheese and Crackers | | 3 Green | 3 Rose | |
| 6—only No. 701—10 in. Hld. Sandwich Plate | | 3 " | 3 " | |
| 6—only No. 701—3 Piece Whipped Cream Set | | 3 " | 3 " | |
| 6—only No. 701—3 Section Covered Relish | | 3 " | 3 " | |
| 6—pairs No. 701—4¾ in. Low Candlesticks | | 3 Prs. " | 3 Prs. " | |
| 6—only No. 701—12 in. Rolled Edge Bowls | | 3 " | 3 " | |

36 Pc. Asst.                Asst. comes in two colors only Rose and Green.

*See other side of folder for individual prices on the above items.*

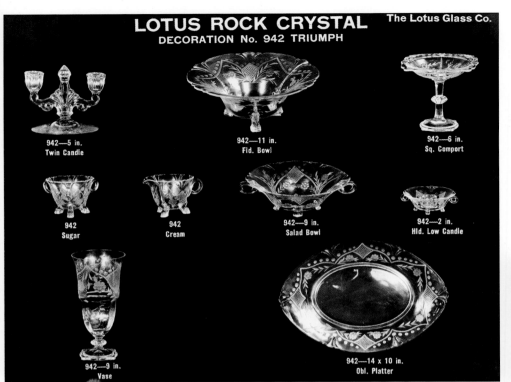

**LOTUS ROCK CRYSTAL** The Lotus Glass Co.
DECORATION No. 942 TRIUMPH

942—5 in.
Twin Candle

942—11 in.
Fld. Bowl

942—6 in.
Sq. Comport

942
Sugar

942
Cream

942—9 in.
Salad Bowl

942—2 in.
Hld. Low Candle

942—9 in.
Vase

942—14 x 10 in.
Obl. Platter

Cutting No. 942 TRIUMPH Pattern.
All crystal. Lotus black and white photograph, linen mounted circa 1940s.
Candle, two light/twin, 5", each $32-42; bowl, 3-footed/console, $40-52;
comport, tall square, 6", $38-48; sugar, $24-28; creamer, $24-28; bowl, salad,
two open handles, footed, $38-48; candle, single low, two open handles, 2",
each $26-36; vase, 9", $48-60; platter oblong, 14" x 10", $42-52.
The Glass Blanks: All pieces shown are Heisey Glass: the candlestick is
Trident No. 84; the bowl is Empress #1401 floral bowl; and the compote,
cream and sugar, both handled bowl and candlestick as well as oval platter
are Empress #1401, the 9" vase is Heisey Saxony line.

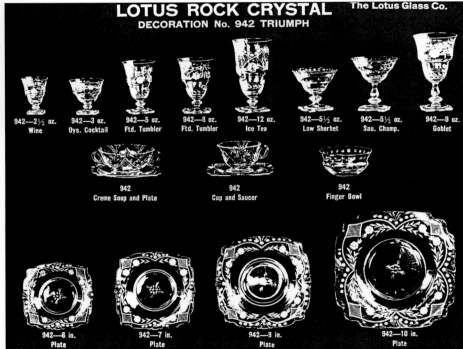

**LOTUS ROCK CRYSTAL** The Lotus Glass Co.
DECORATION No. 942 TRIUMPH

942—2½ oz.
Wine

942—3 oz.
Oys. Cocktail

942—5 oz.
Ftd. Tumbler

942—8 oz.
Ftd. Tumbler

942—12 oz.
Ice Tea

942—5½ oz.
Low Sherbet

942—5½ oz.
Sau. Champ.

942—9 oz.
Goblet

942
Creme Soup and Plate

942
Cup and Saucer

942
Finger Bowl

942—6 in.
Plate

942—7 in.
Plate

942—8 in.
Plate

942—10 in.
Plate

Cutting No. 942 TRIUMPH Pattern.
All crystal. Lotus catalog page circa 1940s.
Wine, 2 1/2 oz., $18-24; cocktail, 3 oz., $14-20; tumbler, footed, 5 oz., $18-24; tumbler, 8
oz., $22-26; ice tea, footed, 12 oz., $26-34; sherbet, low, 5 1/2 oz., $18-24; champagne, 5 1/2
oz., $18-24; goblet, 9 oz., $26-34; crème soup and plate, $26-34; cup and saucer, $22-30;
finger bowl, $18-22; plate, 6", $22-28; plate, 7", $28-32; plate, 8", $32-38; plate, 10", $75-85.
The Glass Blanks: All pieces on this page are Heisey Empress blanks.

## LOTUS ROCK CRYSTAL
### The Lotus Glass Co.
### DECORATION No. 943 MAYFAIR

943—5 in. Twin Candle

943—11 in. Fld. Bowl

943—6 in. Sq. Comport

943 Sugar

943 Cream

943—9 in. Salad Bowl

943—2 in. Hld. Low Candle

943—9 in. Vase

943—14 x 10 in. Obl. Platter

## GREY CUTTING 1124-H "HELEN"
### OPTIC CRYSTAL

5½ oz. Low Sherbet

3½ oz. Footed Tumbler

10 oz. Footed Tumbler

12 oz. Footed Ice Te

12 oz. Pilsener

¾ oz. Cordial

Fruit Salad

9 oz. Goblet

7 oz. Hollow Stem Saucer Champagne

5 oz. Saucer Champagne

3½ oz. Cocktail

5 oz. Claret

4 pt. Jug

14 oz. Handled Beer Mug

8 in. Octagon Plate (also made in 6 in. and 7½ in. sizes)

### "HELEN" Grey Cutting
### OPTIC CRYSTAL

| DOZ. TO CARTON | | | PER DOZEN OPEN STOCK | FULL CARTON |
|---|---|---|---|---|
| 6 | 9 oz. | Goblet | $5.50 | $4.80 |
| 6 | 5½ oz. | Saucer Champagne | 5.50 | 4.80 |
| 6 | 5½ oz. | Low Sherbet | 5.50 | 4.80 |
| 6 | 5 oz. | Claret | 5.50 | 4.80 |
| 6 | 3½ oz. | Cocktail | 5.50 | 4.80 |
| 6 | 2½ oz. | Wine | 5.50 | 4.80 |
| 6 | ¾ oz. | Cordial | 5.50 | 4.80 |
| 6 | 1½ oz. | Sherry | 5.50 | 4.80 |
| 6 | 5 oz. | Claret | 5.50 | 4.80 |
| 6 | 1 oz. | Brandy | 5.50 | 4.80 |
| 6 | 7 oz. | H.S. Sau. Champagne | 5.50 | 4.80 |
| 6 | 5 oz. | H.S. Champagne | 5.50 | 4.80 |
| 6 | | Parfait | 5.50 | 4.80 |
| 6 | | Fruit Salad | 5.50 | 4.80 |
| 6 | 12 oz. | Footed Ice Tea | 5.50 | 4.80 |
| 6 | 10 oz. | Footed Tumbler | 5.50 | 4.80 |
| 6 | 5 oz. | Footed Tumbler | 5.50 | 4.80 |
| 6 | 3½ oz. | Footed Tumbler | 5.50 | 4.80 |
| 3 | 8 in. | Octagon Plate | 7.20 | 6.60 |
| 3 | 7½ in. | Octagon Plate | 6.60 | 6.00 |
| 3 | 6 in. | Octagon Plate | 6.60 | 4.80 |
| 3 | 14 oz. | Hld. Beer Mug | 5.50 | 4.80 |
| 1 | 4 pt. | Jug | 19.20 | 18.00 |
| 3 | 12 oz. | Pilsener | 6.20 | 5.50 |

(Plus Package Charge)

Less Discount

---

Cutting No. 943 MAYFAIR Pattern.
All crystal. Lotus linen backed photograph for catalog circa 1940s.
Candle, two light/twin, 5", each $32-42; bowl, 3-footed/console, $40-52; comport, tall square, 6", $38-48; sugar, $24-28; creamer, $24-28; bowl, salad, two open handles, footed, $38-48; candle, single low, two open handles, 2", each $26-36; vase, 9", $48-60; platter, oblong, 14" x 10", $42-52.
The Glass Blanks: All pieces shown are Heisey Glass: the candlestick is Trident No. 84; the bowl is Empress #1401 floral bowl; and the compote, cream and sugar, both handled bowl and candlestick as well as oval platter are Empress #1401, the 9" vase is Heisey Saxony line.

Cutting No. 1124-H HELEN Pattern.
Crystal with gray or unpolished cutting. Lotus catalog supplement page circa 1930-40s.
Pilsner, $10-16; sherbet, $6-10; tumbler, footed, 3 1/2 oz., $6-10; tumbler, footed, 10 oz., $8-12; ice tea, footed, 12 oz., $12-16; goblet, 9 oz., $14-18; cordial, 3/4 oz., $10-16; champagne, hollow stem, $20-24; champagne, saucer, $8-14; fruit salad, $6-12; cocktail, 3 1/2 oz., $6-10; claret, 5 oz., $10-14; jug, 4 pint, $35-40; beer mug, handled, $12-16; plate, octagon, 8", $10-12.

# Presents

# HOSTESS

*Polished Rock Crystal Cutting*

*N*ow, for that enchanted evening of delightful dining, *LOTUS* master craftsman have created another stunning design in sparkling, rock crystal . . . HOSTESS, for the particular person who wants exceptional beauty in fine glassware that fits perfectly with any silver or chinaware service.

Hostess is a notable addition to the magnificent line of *LOTUS* patterns that are so popular with women everywhere. New brides are finding out and homemakers understand that nothing adds so much beauty and sophisticated decor to an exquisitely set table than hand cut, polished rock crystal, hand made from clear ringing, lead glass.

Hand Made and Hand Cut by

# Lotus

*Creators of Fine Glassware Since 1912*

Cutting No. 7517 Rock Crystal HOSTESS Pattern
Crystal. Lotus point of purchase retail pamphlet circa 1930-40s.
Plate, $10-18; cocktail, $8-12; sherbet, $10-14; goblet, $16-24; tumbler, footed, $12-16.

### ROCK CRYSTAL CUTTING

#### NO. 7519 "ELEANOR"

Lead Glass (Optic)

| No. | | | Per Dozen |
|---|---|---|---|
| 7519—9 | oz. | Goblet | $10.80 |
| 7519—5½ | oz. | Saucer Champagne | 10.80 |
| 7519—6 | oz. | Hollow Stem Saucer Champagne | 12.00 |
| 7519—5½ | oz. | Low Sherbet | 10.80 |
| 7519—5 | oz. | Claret | 10.50 |
| 7519—3½ | oz. | Cocktail | 10.50 |
| 7519—2½ | oz. | Wine | 10.50 |
| 7519—2 | oz. | Sherry | 10.50 |
| 7519—1 | oz. | Brandy | 10.50 |
| 7519—¾ | oz. | Cordial | 10.50 |
| 7519—3½ | oz. | Oyster Cocktail | 10.80 |
| 7519— | | Fruit Salad or Finger Bowl | 12.00 |
| 7519—12 | oz. | Footed Ice Tea | 10.80 |
| 7519—10 | oz. | Footed Tumbler | 10.80 |
| 7519—5 | oz. | Footed Tumbler | 10.50 |
| 7519—3½ | oz. | Footed Tumbler | 10.50 |
| 7519—8 | in. | Salad Plate | 18.00 |
| 7519—7½ | in. | Salad Plate | 18.00 |
| 7519—7½ | in. | Salad Plate | 16.80 |
| 7519—6 | in. | Bread and Butter Plate | 16.20 |
| 4919— | | Sugar and Cream | 30.00 |
| 7119—7 | in. | Tall Comport | 30.00 |
| 23319—11 | in. | 2-Handled Sandwich | 45.00 |
| 23519—12 | in. | Console Bowl | 48.00 |
| 24019—5 | in. | Candlestick | 21.00 |

*Plus Package Charge*

*Less Discount*

Cutting 7519
Eleanor

Cutting No. 7519 Rock Crystal ELEANOR Pattern
Crystal. Lotus point of purchase retail pamphlet circa 1930-40s.
Sherbet, $8-12; goblet, $16-22; tumbler, footed, $12-18; mug, handled beer, $12-18.

## 8044
## MODERNE DESIGN

### Crystal Plain
### LEAD GLASS
### Rock Crystal Cuttings

| No. | | Per Doz. |
|---|---|---|
| 80— 9 | oz. Goblets | $10.80 |
| 80— 5½ | oz. Sherbet | 10.80 |
| 80— 5 | oz. Claret | 10.80 |
| 80— 3½ | oz. Cocktail | 10.80 |
| 80— 2½ | oz. Wine | 10.80 |
| 80— ¾ | oz. Cordial | 10.80 |
| 80— 3½ | oz. Oyster Cocktail | 10.80 |
| 80— | Fruit Salad/Finger Bowl | 10.80 |
| 80—12 | oz. Ftd. Ice Tea | 10.80 |
| 80— 9 | oz. Ftd. Tumbler | 10.80 |
| 80— 6 | oz. Ftd. Tumbler | 10.80 |
| 80— 4 | oz. Ftd. Tumbler | 10.80 |
| 80— 2¾ | oz. Ftd. Tumbler | 10.80 |
| 80— 6 | in. B & B Plate | 16.20 |
| 80— 7½ | in. Salad Plate | 16.80 |
| 80— 8 | in. Salad Plate | 18.00 |
| 80— | Sugar & Cream | 30.00 |
| 80— 7 | in. Tall Comport | 30.00 |
| 80—11 | in. 2-Hld. Sandwich | 45.00 |
| 80—12 | in. Console Bowl | 48.00 |
| 80— 5 | in. Candlestick | 21.00 |

(*Plus Package Charge*)

Less Discount

Cutting 8044 MODERNE DESIGN pattern
All Crystal. Lotus point of purchase retail pamphlet circa 1930-40s.
Plate, salad, $12-18; sherbet, $10-14; cocktail, $8-12; ice tea, $16-20;
cordial, $24-30; goblet, $20-24.
The Glass Blanks: The stemware blanks appear in a Bryce Glass of Mt.
Pleasant, Pennsylvania, catalog circa 1930s.

Cutting No. D - DELORIS PATTERN
All crystal. Lotus catalog circa 1937-38.
Saucer champagne/tall sherbet, 5 oz., $4-6; sherbet, low, 5 oz., $4-6; claret, 5 oz., $6-8;
cocktail, 3 1/2 oz., $4-6; wine, 2 1/2 oz., $6-8; cordial, 1 oz., $10-14; oyster cocktail, footed,
3 1/2 oz., $4-6; bowl, fruit salad, footed, $4-6; saucer champagne, hollow stem, 6 oz., $12-
16; champagne, hollow stem, 5 oz., $10-14; iced tea, footed, 12 oz., $8-10; tumbler, footed,
10 oz., $5-8; tumbler, footed, 5 oz., $4-6; tumbler, footed, 3 1/2 oz., $3-5; tumbler, half
sham, 12 oz., $6-10; tumbler, half sham, 10 oz., $4-8; old fashion, 8 oz., $4-6; Hi ball,
sham, 7 oz., $3-5; toddy, sham, 5 oz., $3-5; whiskey, sham, 1 1/2 oz., $6-8; jug, oval, 4 pt.,
$36-48; ice tub with tab handles, $28-32; bitter bottle w/ metal stopper, $18-28; pilsner, 12
oz., $10-12; jug, 4 pt., $30-42; cocktail shaker with metal lid, $34-42; plate, octagonal
salad, 7 1/2", $5-8; 6" plate (not shown), $4-6; 8" plate (not shown), $6-10.

Cutting No. N

All Crystal. Lotus three-fold brochure for direct mailing, reverse is addressed, etc. The text on the sheet's reverse says, "Lotus products have been well known for 23 years" so this is circa 1935.

Bowl, 2 handled, 9", $12-16; plate, sandwich, two handled, 11", $10-14; relish, 3 part divided with handles, 10", $16-20; relish, 3 part divided, 11", $12-16; bowl, three-toed, flared, 11", $12-16; mayonnaise set, 3 piece, $16-18; candle stick, 3 light, each $28-38; bowl, three-toed, crimped, 11", $12-16; candy box, 3 part with lid, 6", $20-24; salver, cake, low-footed, 12", $28-32; sugar, $6-8; creamer, $6-8; cheese and cracker, two part, 10 1/2", $14-18.

The Glass Blanks: The 3 light candlesticks are Paden City line 890 Crow's Foot. The finial on the covered round candy is also in the manner of Crow's foot but the illustrations, which appear to be drawings, leave some doubt.

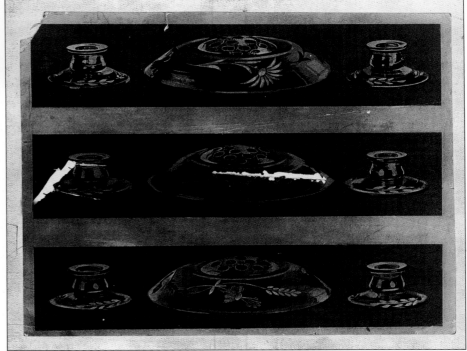

Cutting, unknown numbers and unknown color of glass. Found glued to back of another catalog photograph. Any of the three gray floral cuttings: Candlestick, each $8-12; rolled edge console bowl with flower frog, $40-48.

THE LOTUS GLASS COMPANY, Barnesville, Ohio, U. S. A.

PINETREE 41
No.503...10"
Bud Vase

HARDY 91
No.504...9¼"
Tall
Candle
Stick

PINETREE 41
No.505....7½"
Sweet Pea Vase

HARDY 91
No.506...9"
Cupped Vase

OXFORD 92
No.507..9½"
Footed Vase

PINETREE 41
No.508....6½"
Footed Compote

OXFORD 92
Low Candlestick

No.173   4½"

OXFORD 92
No.510...8"
Footed Center Bowl

HARDY 91
No.511...8"
Globe Vase

OXFORD 92
No.512...9"
Globe Vase

HARDY 91
No.513...12"
Globe Vase

Cutting various numbers. HARDY, PINE TREE, and OXFORD Patterns.
Crystal. Lotus catalog photograph, linen backed. Circa 1940s.
Bud vase, 10", "Pine Tree Cut No. 41", $16-26; candle stick, tall, 9 1/4", "Hardy Cut No. 91", $30-40 each; sweet pea vase, 7 1/2", "Pine Tree Cut No. 41", $22-28; vase, cupped, 9", "Hardy Cut No. 91", $8-14; vase, footed, 9 1/2", "Oxford Cut No. 92", $12-18; comport, footed, 6 1/2", "Pine tree Cut No. 41", $22-28; candlestick, low, 4 1/2", "Oxford Cut No. 92", $12-22; bowl, footed center, 8", "Oxford Cut No. 92", $18-26; globe vase, 8", "Hardy Cut No. 91", $14-24; globe vase, 9", "Oxford Cut No. 92", $14-24; globe vase, 12", "Hardy Cut No. 91", $18-32.

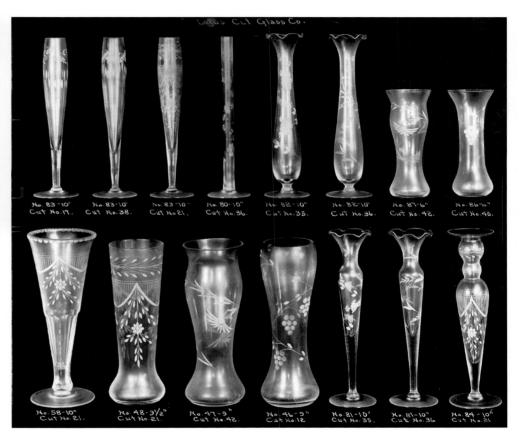

Lotus Cut Glass Co.

No. 83-10"
Cut No. 17.

No. 83-10"
Cut No. 38.

No. 83-10"
Cut No.21.

No. 80-10"
Cut No. 36.

No. 82-10"
Cut No. 35.

No. 82-10"
Cut No. 36.

No. 87-6"
Cut No. 42.

No. 86-6"
Cut No. 40.

No. 58-10"
Cut No. 21.

No. 48-3½"
Cut No. 21.

No. 47-9"
Cut No. 42.

No. 46-9"
Cut No.12.

No. 81-10"
Cut No. 35.

No. 81-10"
Cut No. 36.

No. 84-10"
Cut No. 21.

Cutting various numbers.
Crystal. Lotus catalog page pre-1924.
Vase, cigar shape, Cut No. 17, 10", $6-12; vase, cigar shape, Cut No. 38, 10", $6-12; vase, cigar shape, Cut No. 21, 10", $8-16; vase, pipe, Cut No. 36, 10", $6-14; vase, crimped, Cut No. 35, 10", $6-12; vase, crimped, Cut No. 36, 10", $6-12; vase, Cut No. 42, 6", $6-12; vase, Cut No. 40, 6", $6-12; vase, trumpet, Cut No. 21, 10", $14-22; vase, bulbous, Cut No. 21, 9 1/2", $12-18; vase, Cut No. 42, 9", $6-12; vase, Cut No. 12, 9", $6-12; vase, crimped, Cut No. 35, 10", $6-12; vase, crimped, Cut No. 36, 10", $6-12; vase/candlestick, Cut No. 21, 10", $30-46 each.

**PITKIN & BROOKS.**
**P. & B. (Jewelers) Rock Crystal Assortment.** St.14.34.

Stadler
CHICAGO
NEW YORK

Candy Box.

2 Pc. Sugar & Cream Set.

3 Pc. Sugar & Cream Set. with Tray.

11 in. Relish Tray.

3 Way Candelabra.

Oval Console Bowl.

3 Way Candelabra.

3 Piece Mayonnaise Set.

9 in. Bowl. 2 Hd.

2 Hd. Cake. 10 3/4 in.

Tall Comport 5 1/2 x 6 1/4.

Center Handle Sandwich Tray. 11 in.

Cutting PITKIN & BROOKS (Jewelers) Rock Crystal Assortment
All crystal. Catalog photograph with linen back, circa 1940s.
Candy box with lid, $20-32; sugar, $12-18; creamer, $12-18; 3 piece sugar & cream set with tray, $26-38 set; relish tray, 11", $10-18; candelabra, 3 light, each $38-45; bowl, oval console, $38-48; mayonnaise, 3 piece set, $22-36; bowl, two handled, 9", $16-24; plate, handled cake, 10 3/4", $16-24; comport, tall, 5 1/2" x 6 1/4", $26-34; tray, center handled sandwich, 11", $16-24.
The Glass Blanks: The 3 way candelabra is Imperial Glass #753 introduced circa 1932.

No. 14. 7 inch Candlestick.
Dozen, $6.00

No. 18. 8 inch Candlestick.
Dozen, $18.00

No. 19. 8 inch Candlestick.
Dozen, $18.00

No. 20. 9½ inch Candlestick.
Dozen, $30.00

No. 16. 9½ inch Candlestick.
Dozen, $15.60

No. 17. 9½ inch Candlestick.
Dozen, $18.00

No. 15. 7½ inch Candlestick.
Dozen, $10.80

Cutting various numbers
All Crystal. Lotus partial catalog page.
Candlesticks, No. 20, 9 1/2", each $16-24; No. 14, 7", each $12-22; No. 16, 9 1/2", each $20-32; No. 18, 8", each $14-22;
No. 17, 9 1/2", each $18-26; No. 19, 8", each $16-22; No. 15, 7 1/2", each $12-22.
The Glass Blanks: Stick 15 is Duncan's #66, stick 16 is Duncan's #67, and stick 17 is Duncan's #58. The blank for
Stick 14 is Westmoreland #1023, stick 18 is Westmoreland #1019, and stick 19 is Westmoreland #1027.

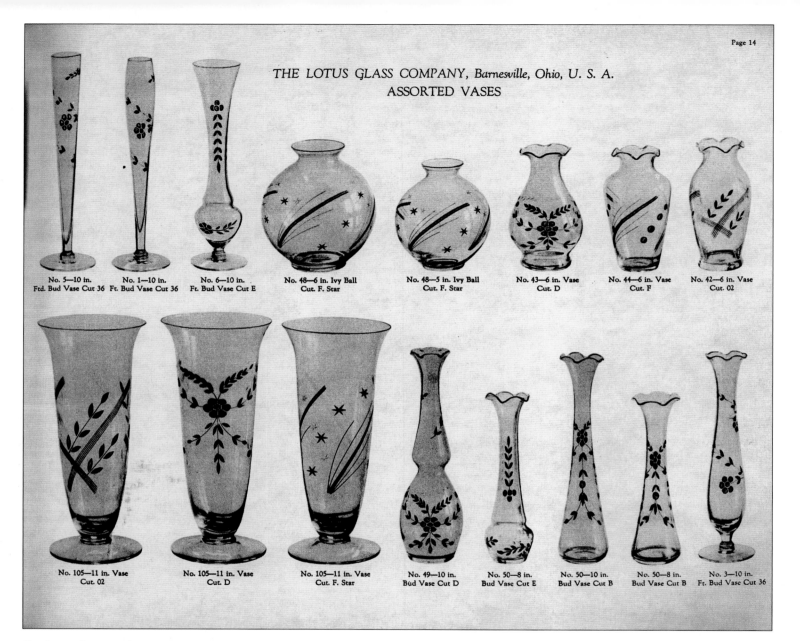

Cutting various numbers
All crystal. Lotus catalog page 1937-38.
All the smaller vases and ivy balls on this page, regardless of shape or
decoration, $4-10. The larger 11"-footed vase, regardless of cut, $10-18.
Vases 42, 44, 49, and others are Weston/West Virginia Glass Specialty shapes
as is the 11"-footed vase. Cambridge also made the 11" vase form.

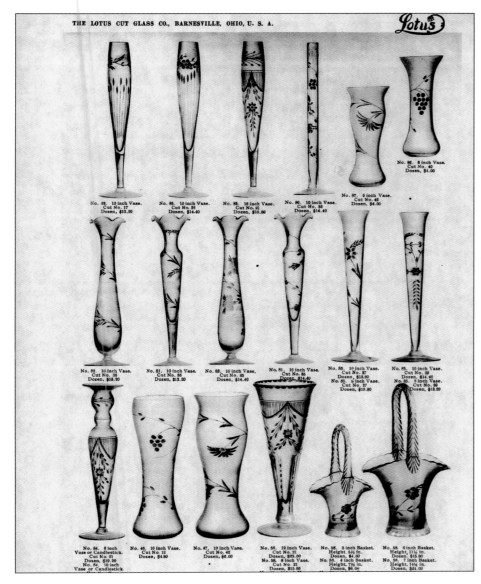

Cutting, various numbers
All crystal. Lotus catalog page pre-1924.
All of these vases appear previously in this chapter under their respective cuttings. Note that several appear to have been in production over a period of several years. Basket cut, 3", $16-22; 4", $20-26; 6", $24-34; 7", $28-38.

Cutting, various number
All crystal. Lotus Cut Glass Co. catalog page pre-1924.
Salt dip, No. 10, $4-10; salt dip, No. 15, $4-12; shaker, pearl top, each $6-8; shaker, glass top, $6-8; shaker, plated top, $4-8; toothpick, Cut No. 36, $4-8; flower block, any size, $4-8; glass spoons, etc., undetermined value; Mayo set, three piece, any illustrated cutting, $18-24; any shown creamer or sugar, each $6-10.

Cuttings 7724 MAJESTIC, 8041 PINETREE, 8151 SPRINGTIME, and 8848 CLASSIC
All crystal. Lotus catalog page circa 1950s.
In any of these patterns the plates are $8-14; footed ice tea, $12-16; goblets, $12-16; wine, $8-12; sherbet, $6-8, cocktails, $6-8.
Note: Some of these patterns are shown more extensively elsewhere in this book, please see the index for the cutting name or number. This page is included as an example of the extensive, high quality cut lines continued by Lotus well into the middle of the century.

No. 7517 Hostess
Crystal Cutting

No. 5447 Windsor
Crystal Cutting

No. 8152 Virginia
Crystal Cutting

No. 6717 Hostess
Crystal Cutting

Cutting 7517 HOSTESS, 5447 WINDSOR, 8152 VIRGINIA, and 6717 HOSTESS
All crystal. Lotus catalog page circa 1950s.
In any of these patterns the plates are $8-14; footed ice tea, $12-16; goblets, $12-16; wine,
$8-12; sherbet, $6-8, cocktails, $6-8.
Note: Some of these patterns are shown more extensively elsewhere in this book, please
see the index for the cutting name or number. This page is included as an example of the
extensive, high quality cut lines continued by Lotus well into the middle of the century.

# Chapter Four

# Etched Patterns with No Gold

Plate Etching No. 0796 LOUISE Pattern
Crystal. Lotus promotional brochure circa 1930s.
Stemware line No. 75, crystal optic.
Plate, salad, $18-22; cocktail, $8-12; low sherbet, $8-12;
goblet, $22-28; and-footed iced tea, $20-26.

**75 Stemware Line**
**Etched Louise 0796**

## Lotus

### 75 STEMWARE LINE
#### CRYSTAL OPTIC
#### Lead Glass
#### "LOUISE" Plate Etching
#### No. 0796

| NO. | | PER DOZ. |
|---|---|---|
| 75—9 oz. | Goblet | $6.00 |
| 75—5½ oz. | Saucer Champ. | 6.00 |
| 75—5½ oz. | Low Sherbet | 6.00 |
| 75—3½ oz. | Cocktail | 5.80 |
| 75—2½ oz. | Wine | 5.80 |
| 75—¾ oz. | Cordial | 5.80 |
| 75— | Fruit Salad | 7.20 |
| 75—12 oz. | Footed Ice Tea | 6.00 |
| 75—10 oz. | Footed Tumbler | 6.00 |
| 75—7 oz. | Footed Tumbler | 5.80 |
| 75—3 oz. | Footed Tumbler | 5.80 |
| 75— | Cup and Saucer | 12.00 |
| 75—10 in. | Plate | 18.00 |
| 75—8 in. | Salad Plate | 13.20 |
| 75—7½ in. | Salad Plate | 10.80 |
| 75—6 in. | Bread and Butter Plate | 7.20 |
| 219—10 in. | Vase | 15.60 |
| 221— | 3-Piece Mayon Set | 15.60 |
| 222—11 in. | Hld. Cake Tray | 14.40 |
| 223— | Sugar and Cream | 16.80 |
| 224—7 in. | 2-Part Candy Box | 12.00 |
| 227—7 in. | Tall Comport | 9.60 |
| 226—5 in. | Tall Candle | 8.40 |
| 228—12 in. | Console Bowl | 16.80 |
| 231—11½ in. | 2-Hld. Sandwich | 12.00 |

Less Discount

Plus Package Charge

THE LOTUS GLASS CO.
BARNESVILLE, OHIO.

LOUISE ETCHING
Nº 0796
ALL CRYSTAL OR
TOPAZ BOWL & CRYSTAL
STEM & FOOT ~

450-9IN.
DINNER PLATE

450-8IN.
SALAD PLATE

450-7½IN.
SALAD PLATE

450 SUGAR & CREAM

450-6IN. BREAD & BUTTER

450
CUP & SAUCER

825
SALT & PEPPER

470-2¾OZ.
FTD. TBLER

470-7OZ.
FTD. TBLER

470-10OZ.
FTD. TBLER

470-12OZ.
FTD. ICE TEA

470-9OZ. GOBLET

470-5½OZ. SAU. CHAMP.

470-5½OZ. LOW SHERBET

470 WINE

470 COCKTAIL

470 CORDIAL

422 FRUIT SALAD

Plate Etching No. 0796 LOUISE Pattern
Topaz with crystal stems and feet. Lotus catalog page circa 1930s.
Plate, dinner, $30-36; plate, salad or luncheon, $24-26; plate, salad, $20-24; sugar, $18-24; creamer, $18-24; plate, bread and butter, $10-14; cup and saucer, $20-26; salt and pepper, each $12-22; footed tumbler, $10-16; footed tumbler, $10-16; footed tumbler, $10-16; iced tea, $16-28; goblet, $28-34; saucer champagne, $12-16; low sherbet, $12-16; wine, $12-16; cocktail, $10-14; cordial, $30-38; bowl, fruit, $12-18.
The Glass Blanks: The stemware is Central Glass line #1470 and the flatware and serving pieces are Central's line #1450. Central closed in bankruptcy in 1939, so this line pre-dates 1939.

Plate Etching No. 905
FUCHSIA Stemware line
76
Crystal. Lotus promotional
brochure circa 1930s.
Goblet, $30-38; iced tea,
$24-32.
The Glass Blanks: The
goblet is Morgantown's
Reverse Twist line #7654.

## FUCHSIA ETCHING No. 0905

### Crystal Optic Only

### 76 Stemware Line

| No. | | | | Per Doz. |
|---|---|---|---|---|
| 76— 9 | oz. | Goblet | | $ 9.90 |
| 76— 5½ | oz. | Tall Sherbet | | 9.90 |
| 76— 5½ | oz. | Low Sherbet | | 9.90 |
| 76— 3½ | oz. | Cocktail | | 9.70 |
| 76— 2½ | oz. | Wine | | 9.70 |
| 76— | | Fruit Salad | | 12.00 |
| 76— 3½ | oz. | Oys. Cocktail | | 9.70 |
| 76—12 | oz. | Ftd. Ice Teas | | 9.90 |
| 76— 9 | oz. | Ftd. Tumbler | | 9.90 |
| 76— 5 | oz. | Ftd. Tumbler | | 9.70 |
| 60—10 | in. | Dinner Plate | | 21.60 |
| 60— 9 | in. | Dinner Plate | | 18.00 |
| 60— 8 | in. | Salad Plate | | 15.60 |
| 60— 7½ | in. | Salad Plate | | 14.40 |
| 60— 6 | in. | B & B Plate | | 13.20 |
| 21 | | Cup & Saucer | | 16.80 |
| 97— 4 | pt. | Jug | | 36.00 |
| 87— | | Sugar & Cream | | 24.00 |
| 200—10 | in. | Hld. Cake | | 24.00 |
| 200 | | Whip Cream Set | | 24.00 |
| 201— 6 | in. | Cov. Candy Box | | 24.00 |
| 205—12 | in. | 6-Toe Bowl | | 24.00 |
| 201— 3½ | in. | Low candles | | 12.00 |

*Less Keystone*

Fuchsia Etching No.0905  Optic - Crystal.                                    c6675

The Lotus Glass Co.
Barnesville, Ohio.

60 - 7 1/2 in.        60 - 8 in.        200 - 3 pc.                 87
Salad Plate.         Salad Plate.      Whip Cream Set.          Sugar & Cream.

76 - 9 oz.   76 - 5 oz.   76 - 5 oz.   76 - 3 oz.   76 - 12 oz.   76 - 10 oz.        21              201 - 6 in.
Goblet.      High         Low          Cocktail.    Ftd.          Ftd.         Cup & Saucer     Cov'd. Candy Box
             Sherbet.     Sherbet.                  Ice Tea.      Tumbler

200 - 10 in. Hld. Cake.   201 - 3 1/2 in.   205 - 12 in.   201 - 3 1/2 in.   87 - 4 pint
                          Low Candle.       6-Toe Bowl.    Low Candle.       Jug.

Plate Etching No. 905 (same as 0905) FUCHSIA Pattern
Crystal only. Original Lotus catalog page circa 1930s.
Plate, salad, 7 1/2", $14-20; plate, salad, 8", $16-20; whip cream set/mayonnaise 3 pieces, $28-38; sugar and
creamer, each $18-24; goblet, 9 oz., $30-38; sherbet, high/saucer champagne, 5 oz., $18-22; sherbet, low, 5 oz.,
$18-22; cocktail, 3 oz., $14-18; ice tea, footed, 12 oz., $24-32; tumbler, footed, 10 oz., $12-16; cup and saucer,
$20-28; candy box with lid, 3 part divided, 6", $32-38; plate, cake/center handled server, 10", $30-38; candle,
low, 3 1/2", each $20-24; bowl, 6-toed, 12", $34-42; jug, 4 pint, $65-80.
Note: The same etching exists with gold, see that chapter for the decoration 905 with gold and relevant pricing.
The Glass Blanks: The stemware line blanks are Morgantown Reverse Twist line #7654.

Plate etching 906 BRIDAL BOUQUET
All crystal. Lotus catalog photograph mounted on linen. Circa 1940s. Mayo w/ under plate, 3 pieces, $38-44; two light candelabrum, each $44-52; bowl, toed, flat rim, $34-42; divided candy box w/ lid, $38-46; compote, $40-48; single candlestick, tall, each $20-24; bowl, toed, $38-42; cake stand, $50-64; bowl, two tab handles, $30-36; cheese and cracker w/ cheese dome, $40-48; center handled server, $30-34; banana bowl, $38-44.
Note: Bridal Bouquet may be the longest and most diverse line produced by Lotus. It can be found on literally dozens of different forms, shapes, and various companies blanks all produced over four decades or more. While it is not yet highly collectible, it has a significant following in the tableware replacement industry due to the longevity of its presence on the market.
The Glass Blanks: Paden City Glass. Included here is a mix of line #211 Spire and Maya line #221 and probably others.

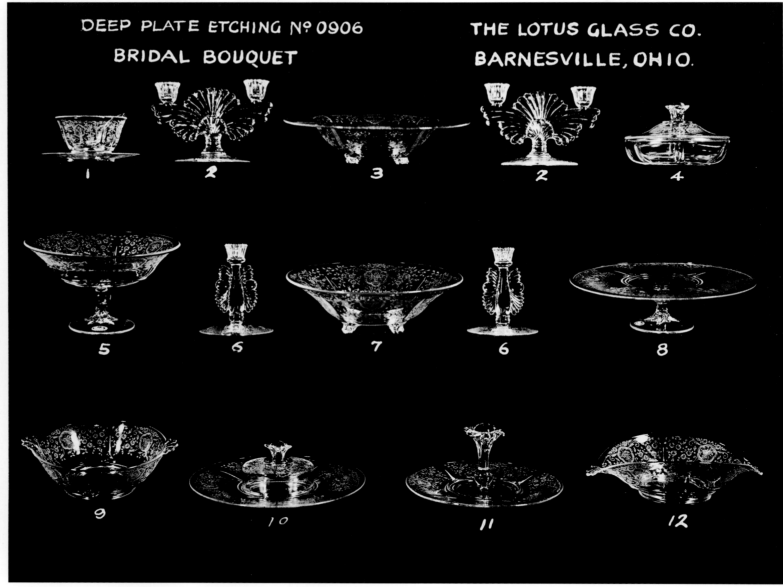

DEEP PLATE ETCHING № 0906
BRIDAL BOUQUET

THE LOTUS GLASS CO.
BARNESVILLE, OHIO.

DEEP PLATE ETCHING Nº 0906
BRIDAL BOUQUET

THE LOTUS GLASS CO.
BARNESVILLE, OHIO

Plate etching 906 BRIDAL BOUQUET
All crystal. Lotus catalog photograph mounted on linen. Circa 1940s.
Torte plate, $38-44; cheese and cracker, two part, $32-38; torte plate, rolled rim,
$38-42; vase, $48-58; five part divided relish, $30-36; cake plate, two handles,
$30-34; cocktail shaker w/ chrome lid, $74-80; torte plate, no pattern in glass,
$38-46; bowl, $32-38; torte plate, no pattern in glass, rolled rim, $34-44.
The Glass Blanks: Paden City Glass. Included here seems to be a mix of Spire
line #211 and Maya line #221, and probably others if they could be examined.
The blown pieces, the footed vase, and cocktail shaker are not Paden City.

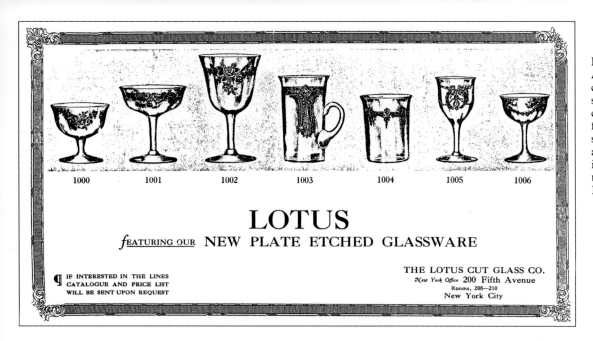

Plate etchings 1000, 1001, 1002, 1003, 1004, 1005, and 1006.

A circa 1910s Lotus ad promoting a variety of plate etchings and offering a catalog. When this ad was readied for this book I wrote a caption, "What a significant contribution to glass scholarship the publication of one such catalog would make today!" Imagine my intense excitement when, in a packet from Don Hanse of the family that owned Lotus so long, a small catalog came showing all of these etchings! These pages, all included in this book, are from a similar catalog to that mentioned in the ad but not the same as the catalog included herein lack etchings 1005 and 1006. Note the pages and this ad refer to Lotus Cut Glass Company, dating them as pre-1924 when the name became Lotus Glass without the word "Cut."

Plate Etching No. 1000 ROSE Pattern Crystal. Original Lotus catalog pre-1924. Cordial, 1 oz., $40-48; wine, 3 oz., $14-20; sherbet, low, $10-14; cocktail, 3 1/2 oz., $10-14; sherbet, high, $10-14; goblet, 9 oz., $22-28; café parfait, $14-18; whiskey, 2 1/2 oz., $22-28; tumbler, 5 oz., $10-14; tumbler, 10 oz., $12-16; ice tea, 12 oz., $12-20; handled ice tea, 12 oz., $14-22.

THE LOTUS CUT GLASS CO., BARNESVILLE, OHIO, U. S. A.

**Lotus**

No. 25
1 oz. Cordial, Optic.

No. 25
Wine, Optic.

No. 25
Low Ftd. Sherbet, Optic.

No. 25
3 oz. Cocktail, Optic.

No. 25
High Ftd. Sherbet, Optic.

No. 25
9 oz. Goblet, Optic.

No. 520-25
Cafe Parfait, Optic.

No. 740
2½ oz. Whiskey, Optic.

No. 740
5 oz. Tumbler, Optic.

No. 740
10 oz. Table Tumbler, Optic.

No. 740
12 oz. Ice Tea Tumbler, Optic.

No. 740
12 oz. Hdl. Ice Tea Tumbler, Optic.

PLATE ETCHING No. 1001          GARLAND PATTERN.          SCALE THREE-EIGHTHS ACTUAL SIZE.

Plate Etching No. 1001 GARLAND Pattern a.k.a. McGUIRE Pattern
Crystal. Original Lotus catalog pre-1924.
Cordial, 1 oz., $40-48; wine, 3 oz., $14-20; sherbet, low, $10-14; cocktail, 3 1/2 oz., $10-12; sherbet, high, $10-14;
goblet, 9 oz., $20-26; café parfait, $12-16; whiskey, 2 1/2 oz., $20-26; tumbler, 5 oz., $8-12; tumbler, 10 oz., $10-
14; ice tea, 12 oz., $10-18; handled ice tea, 12 oz., $14-22.
Note: The etching line numbered 1001 was in production for some time and named Garland by Lotus. Author
Hazel Marie Weatherman in her depression glass book renamed it McGuire. Note that Seneca Glass and other
American companies and at least one Bohemian company also made plate etched decoration very similar to this.

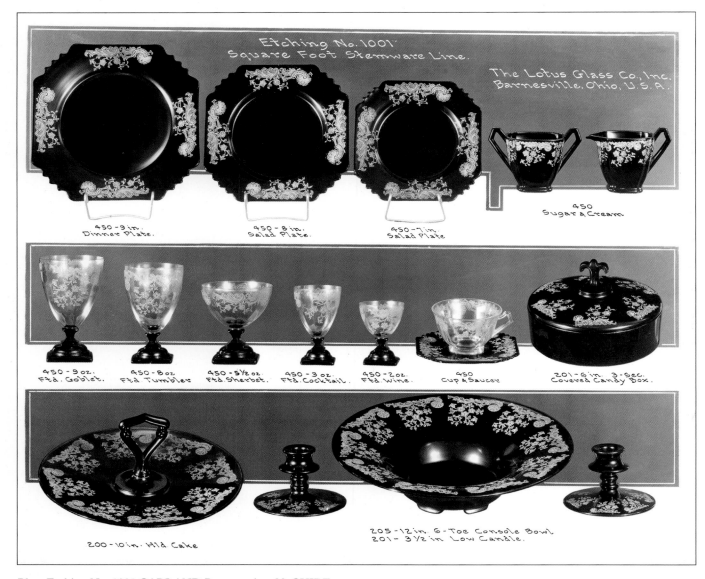

Plate Etching No. 1001 GARLAND Pattern a.k.a. McGUIRE
Black glass and black w/ crystal.
Plate, dinner, $48-58; plate, salad/luncheon, $28-38; plate, salad, $26-36; sugar, $40-55; creamer, $40-55; footed goblet, $38-48; footed tumbler, $34-40; footed sherbet, $30-38; footed cocktail, $28-36; footed wine, $30-38; cup and saucer, $48-58; covered candy w/ lid, $130-150; center handled server/cake, $58-75; candlestick, low, each $40-48; console bowl, six-toed, $85-110.
The Glass Blanks: All Central Glass Works. Plates and stemware are Central's line 1450. The candy box is line #2005, the low candles are #2000, and the footed bowl is #2014.
Note: The etching line numbered 1001 was in production for some time and named Garland by Lotus. Author Hazel Marie Weatherman in her depression glass book renamed it McGuire.

No. 492
1 oz. Cordial, Optic.

No. 492
3 oz. Wine, Optic.

No. 492
Low Sherbet, Optic.

No. 492
3½ oz. Cocktail, Optic.

No. 492
9 oz. High Sherbet, Optic.

No. 492
9 oz. Goblet, Optic.

No. 520
Cafe Parfait, Optic.

No. 740
2½ oz. Whiskey, Optic.

No. 740
5 oz. Tumbler, Optic.

No. 740
10 oz. Table Tumbler, Optic.

No. 740
12 oz. Ice Tea Tumbler, Optic.

No. 740
12 oz. Hdl. Ice Tea Tumbler, Optic.

PLATE ETCHING No. 1002      AMERICAN BEAUTY PATTERN.      SCALE THREE-EIGHTHS ACTUAL SIZE.

Plate Etching No. 1002 AMERICAN BEAUTY Pattern
Crystal. Original Lotus catalog pre-1924.
Cordial, 1 oz., $40-48; wine, 3 oz., $12-16; sherbet, low, $10-14; cocktail, 3 1/2 oz., $10-16; sherbet, high,
$12-16; goblet, 9 oz., $24-32; café parfait, $16-20; whiskey, 2 1/2 oz., $20-28; tumbler, 5 oz., $8-14;
tumbler, 10 oz., $12-18; ice tea, 12 oz., $14-22; handled ice tea, 12 oz., $16-24.

THE LOTUS CUT GLASS CO., BARNESVILLE, OHIO, U. S. A.

No. 520
1 oz. Cordial, Optic.

No. 520
2½ oz. Wine, Optic.

No. 520
Low Sherbet, Optic.

No. 520
3 oz. Cocktail, Optic.

No. 520
High Sherbet, Optic.

No. 520
9 oz. Goblet, Optic.

No. 25
6 oz. Cafe Parfait, Optic.

No. 740
2½ oz. Whiskey, Optic.

No. 740
5 oz. Tumbler, Optic.

No. 740
10 oz. Table Tumbler, Optic.

No. 740
12 oz. Ice Tea Tumbler, Optic.

No. 740
12 oz. Hdl. Ice Tea Tumbler, Optic

PLATE ETCHING No. 1003

MARTHA PATTERN.

SCALE THREE-EIGHTHS ACTUAL SIZE.

Plate Etching No. 1003 MARTHA Pattern
Crystal. Original Lotus catalog pre-1924.
Cordial, 1 oz., $40-48; wine, 3 oz., $12-26; sherbet, low, $10-14; cocktail, 3 1/2 oz., $10-14; sherbet, high,
$10-14; goblet, 9 oz., $22-38; café parfait, $14-18; whiskey, 2 1/2 oz., $20-28; tumbler, 5 oz., $8-14;
tumbler, 10 oz., $10-16; ice tea, 12 oz., $12-20; handled ice tea, 12 oz., $14-22.

No. 520. 1 oz.
Cordial, Optic.

No. 520
2½ oz. Wine, Optic.

No. 520
Low Sherbet, Optic

No. 520
3 oz. Cocktail, Optic.

No. 520
High Sherbet, Optic.

No. 520
9 oz. Goblet, Optic.

No. 520
6 oz. Cafe Parfait, Optic.

No. 740
2½ oz. Whiskey, Optic.

No. 740
5 oz. Tumbler, Optic.

No. 740
10 oz. Table Tumbler, Optic.

No. 740
12 oz. Ice Tea Tumbler, Optic.

No. 740
12 oz. Hdl. Ice Tea Tumbler, Optic

PLATE ETCHING No. 1004     CLEO PATTERN.     SCALE THREE-EIGHTHS ACTUAL SIZE.

Plate Etching No. 1004 CLEO Pattern
Crystal. Original Lotus catalog pre-1924.
Cordial, 1 oz., $22-30; wine, 3 oz., $12-18; sherbet, low, $10-14; cocktail, 3 1/2 oz., $8-12; sherbet, high, $10-14; goblet, 9 oz., $20-26; café parfait, $10-14; whiskey, 2 1/2 oz., $20-24; tumbler, 5 oz., $8-12; tumbler, 10 oz., $10-14; ice tea, 12 oz., $10-16; handled ice tea, 12 oz., $12-20.

## Optic Plate Etching No. 1007

No. 500
5 1/2 oz.
High Sherbet
$3.60 Doz.

No. 840—9 oz.
Table Tumbler
$2.50 Doz.

No. 106
Grape Juice Jug
and Cover
$13.20 Doz.

No. 500
5 1/2 oz.
Low Sherbet
$3.60 Doz.

No. 840—12 oz. Ice
Tea Tumbler
$2.85 Doz.

No. 105—54 oz. Jug
$12.00 Doz.

No. 840
5 oz.
Tumbler
$2.50 Doz.

No. 109—Ice Tea Jug
and Cover
$14.40 Doz.

No. 500
3 1/2 oz.
Cocktail
$3.50 Doz.

No. 500
9 oz. Goblet
$3.60 Doz.

No. 500
2 1/2 oz. Wine
$3.50 Doz.

Plate etching 1007
Crystal. Original Lotus catalog page found glued to reverse of another page, circa 1920s.
Condition of illustration as found.
Sherbet, high, $8-14; jug, grape juice with lid, $32-36; sherbet, low, $8-12; tumbler, 5 oz., $6-10; jug, iced tea with lid, $40-48; tumbler, table, 9 oz., $10-14; tumbler, tea, 12 oz., $10-14; jug, $30-36; cocktail, 3 1/2 oz., $6-10; goblet, 9 oz., $16-24; wine, 2 1/2 oz., $12-16.

*Opposite Page:*
Plate Etching No. 1011 FLANDERS Pattern.
Crystal or topaz. Lotus catalog photograph mounted on linen circa 1930-40s.
Show and priced in crystal only. Topaz as noted on page, add 20-40%.
Footed iced tea, $16-22; footed tumbler, 10 oz., $12-16; footed tumbler, 5 oz., $8-14; footed tumbler, 3 oz., $8-14; claret, $10-16; wine, $10-16; cocktail, $8-14; saucer champagne, $8-14; low sherbet, $8-14; plate, salad, 6", $10-14; cordial, $24-32; parfait, $10-14; bowl, fruit, $10-14; plate, dinner, 8", $18-24; plate, salad/luncheon, 7 1/2", $12-16; goblet, $18-24; jug/pitcher, $80-95.

Furnished in
Crystal or Topaz.

"FLANDERS" Etching No. 1011.
No. 66 Line Optic.

C512-1

66-12 oz.
Ftd. Ice Tea.

66-10 oz.
Ftd. Tumbler.

66-5 oz.
Ftd. Tumbler.

66-3 oz.
Ftd. Tumbler.

66-5 oz.
Claret.

66-2½ oz.
Wine.

66-3½ oz.
Cocktail.

66-5½ oz.
Sau. Champ.

66-5½ oz.
Low Sherbet.

66-6 in.
Oct. Plate.

66-¾ oz.
Cordial.

66-5 oz.
Parfait.

66-
Fruit Salad.

66-8 in.
Oct. Plate.

66-7½ in.
Oct. Plate.

66-9 oz.
Goblet.

66-4 Pt.
Jug.

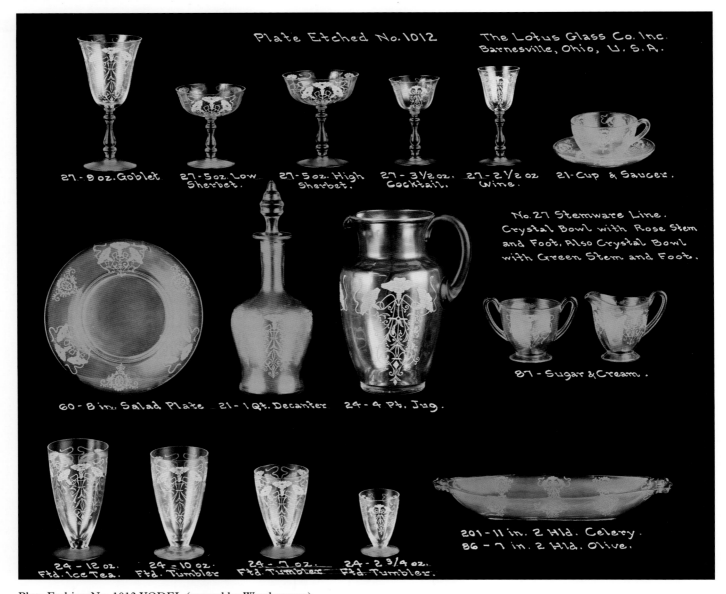

Plate Etched No. 1012    The Lotus Glass Co. Inc. Barnesville, Ohio, U.S.A.

27 - 9 oz. Goblet.
27 - 5 oz. Low Sherbet.
27 - 5 oz. High Sherbet.
27 - 3½ oz. Cocktail.
27 - 2½ oz. Wine.
21 - Cup & Saucer.

No. 27 Stemware Line. Crystal Bowl with Rose Stem and Foot. Also Crystal Bowl with Green Stem and Foot.

60 - 8 in. Salad Plate
21 - 1 Qt. Decanter
24 - 4 Pt. Jug.
87 - Sugar & Cream.

24 - 12 oz. Ftd. Ice Tea.
24 - 10 oz. Ftd. Tumbler.
24 - 7 oz. Ftd. Tumbler.
24 - 2¾ oz. Ftd. Tumbler.
201 - 11 in. 2 Hld. Celery.
86 - 7 in. 2 Hld. Olive.

Plate Etching No. 1012 YODEL (named by Weatherman)
Crystal and pink or crystal and green combinations as illustrated. Serving pieces in green or pink. Lotus catalog photograph, hand-colored and mounted on linen. Circa 1930s.
Goblet, $22-29; sherbet, low, $12-16; sherbet, high/saucer champagne, $12-16; cocktail, $12-16; wine, $12-18; cup and saucer, $22-30; plate, salad, $14-22; decanter w/ stopper, $95-110; jug/pitcher, $80-95; sugar, $18-26; creamer, $18-26; footed iced tea, $22-29; footed tumbler, 10 oz., $14-20; footed tumbler, 7 oz., $12-18; footed tumbler, 2 3/4 oz., $12-16; celery, two handled, 11", $26-34; celery, two handled, 7", $20-28.
The Glass Blanks: The decanter is Central Glass, the jug may be Weston.

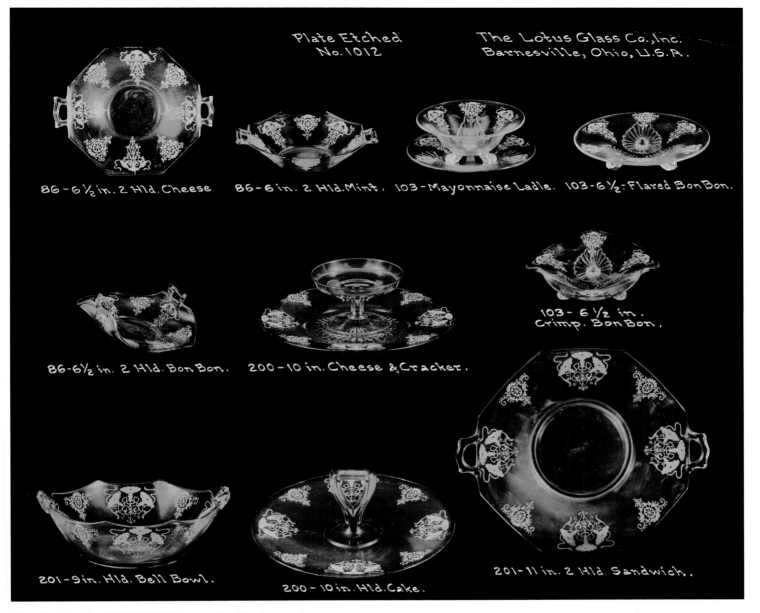

Plate Etched No. 1012

The Lotus Glass Co., Inc.
Barnesville, Ohio, U.S.A.

86 – 6½ in. 2 Hld. Cheese

86 – 6 in. 2 Hld. Mint.

103 – Mayonnaise Ladle.

103 – 6½ – Flared Bon Bon.

86 – 6½ in. 2 Hld. Bon Bon.

200 – 10 in. Cheese & Cracker.

103 – 6½ in. Crimp. Bon Bon.

201 – 9 in. Hld. Bell Bowl.

200 – 10 in. Hld. Cake.

201 – 11 in. 2 Hld. Sandwich.

Plate Etching No. 1012 YODEL (named by Weatherman)
Pink and Green. Lotus catalog photograph hand-colored and mounted on linen. Circa 1930s.
Cheese/cake, two open handles, $22-28; mint, two open handles, $18-26; mayonnaise with under plate, $24-28; bonbon, three-toed, flared, $16-22; bonbon, two open handles, $16-24; cheese and cracker, two piece, $22-28; bonbon, three-toed, crimped, $16-22; bowl, two open handles, $24-34; center handled server, $22-32; sandwich tray, two open handles, $24-30.
The Glass Blanks: the mayo and two bonbons are Duncan & Miller Three-Leaf line circa 1929.

## PLATE ETCHED No. 1012

### No. 27 Stemware Line

**Crystal Bowl with Rose Stem and Foot,
also Crystal Bowl with Green Stem and Foot.**

#### (OPTIC)

| No. | | | | Per Doz. |
|---|---|---|---|---|
| 27— 9 | oz. | Goblet | | $ 8.00 |
| 27— 5 | oz. | High Sherbet | | 8.00 |
| 27— 5 | oz. | Low Sherbet | | 8.00 |
| 27— 2½ | oz. | Wine | | 7.80 |
| 27— 3½ | oz. | Cocktail | | 7.80 |
| 24—12 | oz. | Ftd. Ice Tea | | 8.00 |
| 24—10 | oz. | Ftd. Tumbler | | 8.00 |
| 24— 7 | oz. | Ftd. Tumbler | | 8.00 |
| 24— 2¾ | oz. | Ftd. Tumbler | | 7.20 |
| 24— 4 | pt. | Jug | | 36.00 |
| 21— 1 | qt. | *Decanter | | 36.00 |
| 21— | | *Cup & Saucer | | 16.00 |
| 60— 6 | in. | *Bread & Butter Plate | | 10.80 |
| 60— 7½ | in. | *Salad Plate | | 13.20 |
| 60— 8 | in. | *Salad Plate | | 14.40 |
| 60— 9 | in. | *Dinner Plate | | 16.80 |
| 60—12 | in. | *Service Plate | | 33.30 |
| 87— | | *Sugar & Cream | | 21.60 |
| 201—11 | in. | *2-Hld. Celery | | 21.60 |
| 200—10 | in. | *Hld. Cake | | 21.60 |
| 201—11 | in. | *2-Hld. Sandwich | | 21.60 |
| 200—10 | in. | *Cheese & Cracker | | 21.60 |
| 201— 9 | in. | *Hld. Bell Bowl | | 21.60 |
| 86— 6 | in. | *2-Hld. Mint | | 13.20 |
| 86— 6½ | in. | *2-Hld. Bon Bon | | 13.20 |
| 86— 6½ | in. | *2-Hld. Cheese | | 13.20 |
| 86— 7 | in. | *2-Hld. Olive | | 13.20 |
| 103— 6½ | in. | *Crimp Bon Bon | | 13.20 |
| 103— 6½ | in. | *Flared Bon Bon | | 13.20 |
| 103— | | *Mayonaise Bowl & Ladle | | 15.60 |

*These items furnished in solid colors only.

**Less Keystone discount**

*Less 50. ✓ 10 %*

Plate Etching No. 1012 YODEL (named by Weatherman)
Lotus point of purchase piece type list with dimensions and pieces produced.
Goblet, $22-29.

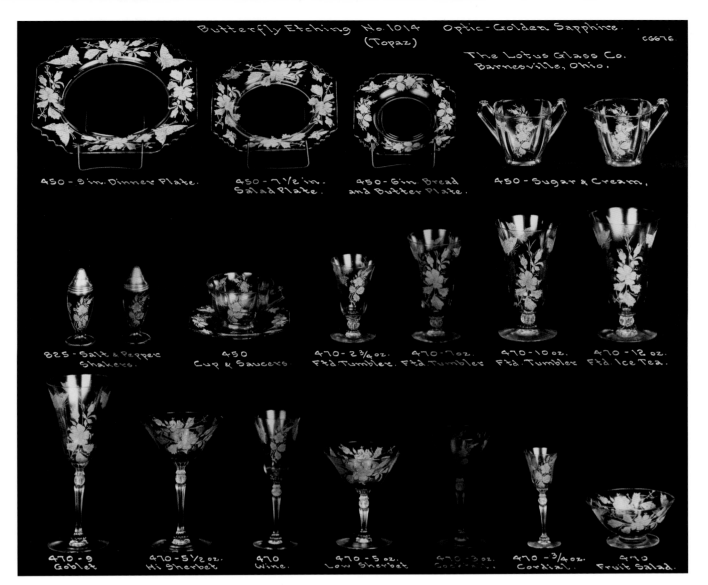

Butterfly Etching No. 1014    Optic-Golden Sapphire.
(Topaz)                                          C6676

The Lotus Glass Co.
Barnesville, Ohio.

450 - 9 in. Dinner Plate.    450 - 7½ in. Salad Plate.    450 - 6 in. Bread and Butter Plate.    450 - Sugar & Cream.

825 - Salt & Pepper Shakers.    450 Cup & Saucers.    470 - 2¾ oz. Ftd Tumbler.    470 - 7 oz. Ftd Tumbler.    470 - 10 oz. Ftd Tumbler.    470 - 12 oz. Ftd. Ice Tea.

470 - 9 Goblet    470 - 5½ oz. Hi Sherbet    470 Wine.    470 - 5 oz. Low Sherbet    470 - 3 oz. Cocktail.    470 - ¾ oz. Cordial.    470 Fruit Salad.

Plate Etching No. 1014 BUTTERFLY Pattern
Golden sapphire/topaz and crystal combinations and serving pieces in golden sapphire. Original catalog photograph hand-colored and mounted on linen. 1930s. Priced as shown for golden sapphire. For crystal deduct 20-35%.
Plate, dinner, $36-48; plate, salad/luncheon, $18-26; plate, bread & butter, $14-20; sugar, $24-32; creamer, $24-32; salt and pepper set, $38-48; cup and saucer, $24-32; footed tumbler, 2 3/4 oz., $12-18; footed tumbler, 7 oz., $14-18; footed tumbler, 10 oz., $14-20; iced tea, $16-24; goblet, $26-36; tall sherbet/saucer champagne, $12-18; wine, $14-20; low sherbet, $12-18; cocktail, $12-18; cordial, $26-38; bowl, fruit, $12-16.
The stem line is Central Glass, as are the plates, creamer, and sugar. Central closed in bankruptcy in 1939, so this pattern predates that time.

**(BUTTERFLY) Etching No. 1014**

**Stemware & Flatware**

## (BUTTERFLY) Plate Etching
## No. 1014
### Stemware & Flatware
#### CRYSTAL OPTIC
### Lead Glass

| NO. | | PER DOZ. |
|---|---|---|
| 470—9 oz. | Goblet | $7.50 |
| 470—5½ oz. | High Sherbet | 7.50 |
| 470—5½ oz. | Low Sherbet | 7.50 |
| 470—3½ oz. | Cocktail | 7.30 |
| 470—2½ oz. | Wine | 7.30 |
| 470—¾ oz. | Cordial | 7.20 |
| 422— | Fruit Salad | 9.60 |
| 470—12 oz. | Footed Ice Tea | 7.50 |
| 470—10 oz. | Footed Tumbler | 7.50 |
| 470—7 oz. | Footed Tumbler | 7.50 |
| 470—2¾ oz. | Footed Tumbler | 7.30 |
| 440— | Cup and Saucer | 16.00 |
| 450—9 in. | Dinner Plate | 16.00 |
| 450—8 in. | Salad Plate | 14.00 |
| 450—7 in. | Salad Plate | 11.00 |
| 450—6 in. | Bread and Butter Plate | 9.00 |
| 450— | Sugar and Cream | 16.80 |
| 825— | Salt and Pepper | 18.00 |
| 205—12 in. | 6-Toe Bowl | 24.00 |
| 201—3½ in. | Low Candle | 10.00 |
| 200—10 in. | Hld. Cake Tray | 20.40 |
| 201—6 in. | 3-Sec. Cov. Candy | 24.00 |
| 200— | 3-pc. Whip. Cream Set | 21.60 |

Less Discount

Plus Package Charge

Plate Etching No. 1014
BUTTERFLY Pattern
Lotus promotional brochure
circa 1930s.
Piece type list with dimensions.
See previous illustration for
prices.

Plate Etching No. 1015 DRESDEN Pattern Crystal or topaz, shown and priced in crystal. Topaz add 20-40%. Lotus catalog page mounted on linen circa 1930-40s.

Footed iced tea, $12-18; footed tumbler, 10 oz., $10-16; footed tumbler, 5 oz., $8-14; footed tumbler, 3 oz., $8-12; claret, $10-16; wine, $10-14; cocktail, $8-12; saucer champagne, $8-12; low sherbet, $8-12; plate, salad, 6", $8-12; cordial, $12-20; parfait, $10-16; bowl, fruit, $8-14; plate, dinner, 8", $10-26; plate, salad/luncheon, 7 1/2", $10-18; goblet, $12-20; jug/pitcher, $45-58.

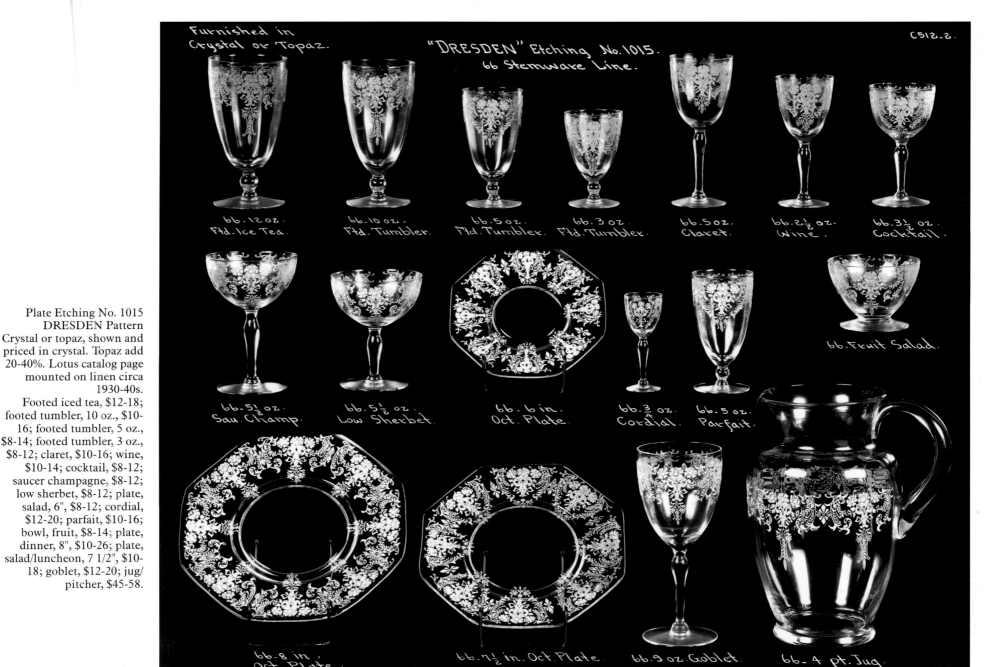

**40 Line**
**Etched 1019**

## *Lotus*

### Plate Etching No. 1019
### NO. 40 LINE
#### CRYSTAL OPTIC

| NO. | | | PER DOZ. |
|---|---|---|---|
| 40—9 oz. | Goblet | | $4.80 |
| 40—5½ oz. | Saucer Champaign | | 4.80 |
| 40—5½ oz. | Low Sherbet | | 4.80 |
| 40—5 oz. | Parfait | | 4.80 |
| 40— | Fruit Salad | | 4.80 |
| 40—5 oz. | Claret | | 4.80 |
| 40—2½ oz. | Wine | | 4.80 |
| 40—3½ oz. | Cocktail | | 4.80 |
| 40—¾ oz. | Cordial | | 4.80 |
| 40—12 oz. | Footed Ice Tea | | 4.80 |
| 40—9 oz. | Footed Tumbler | | 4.80 |
| 40—6 oz. | Footed Tumbler | | 4.80 |
| 40—3½ oz. | Footed Tumbler | | 4.80 |
| 40—8 in. | Salad Plate | | 7.70 |
| 40—7½ in. | Salad Plate | | 7.50 |
| 40—6 in. | B. & B. Plate | | 7.30 |
| 40—14 oz. | Hld. Beer Mug | | 4.80 |

Less Discount

Plus Package Charge

Plate Etching No. 1019
Crystal optic. Lotus promotional brochure circa 1930-40s.
Beer mug, handled, $18-22; jug/pitcher, $65-78; goblet, $18-24; saucer champagne/sherbet, $14-19; iced tea, $16-22.

**75 Stemware Line**
**Etched Thelma 1023**

## *Lotus*

### 75 STEMWARE LINE
#### CRYSTAL OPTIC
#### Lead Glass
### "THELMA" Plate Etching
### No. 1023

| NO. | | | PER DOZ. |
|---|---|---|---|
| 75—9 oz. | Goblet | | $6.00 |
| 75—5½ oz. | Saucer Champ. | | 6.00 |
| 75—5½ oz. | Low Sherbet | | 6.00 |
| 75—3½ oz. | Cocktail | | 5.80 |
| 75—2½ oz. | Wine | | 5.80 |
| 75—¾ oz. | Cordial | | 5.80 |
| 75— | Fruit Salad | | 7.20 |
| 75—12 oz. | Footed Ice Tea | | 6.00 |
| 75—10 oz. | Footed Tumbler | | 6.00 |
| 75—7 oz. | Footed Tumbler | | 5.80 |
| 75—3 oz. | Footed Tumbler | | 5.80 |
| 75— | Cup and Saucer | | 12.00 |
| 75—10 in. | Plate | | 18.00 |
| 75—8 in. | Salad Plate | | 13.20 |
| 75—7½ in. | Salad Plate | | 10.80 |
| 75—6 in. | Bread and Butter Plate | 7.20 |
| 219—10 in. | Vase | | 15.60 |
| 221— | 3-Piece Mayon Set | | 15.60 |
| 222—11 in. | Hld. Cake Tray | | 14.40 |
| 223— | Sugar and Cream | | 16.80 |
| 224—7 in. | 2-Part Candy Box | | 12.00 |
| 227—7 in. | Tall Comport | | 9.60 |
| 226—5 in. | Tall Candle | | 8.40 |
| 228—12 in. | Console Bowl | | 16.80 |
| 231—11½ in. | 2-Hld. Sandwich | | 12.00 |

Less Discount

Plus Package Charge

Plate Etching No. 1023 THELMA Pattern
Crystal. Stemware line No. 75. Lotus promotional brochure circa 1930-40s.
Plate, salad, $14-22; cocktail, $10-14; sherbet, $12-16; iced tea, $18-24; goblet, $20-26.

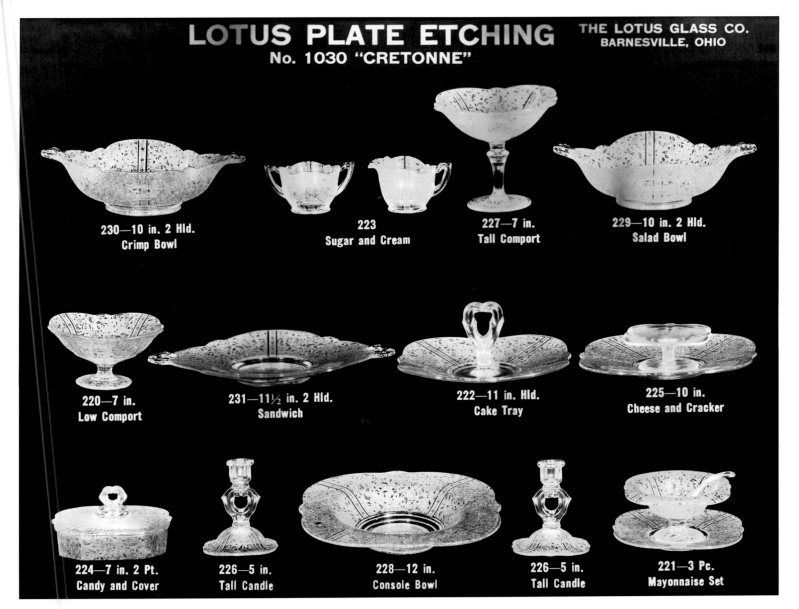

## LOTUS PLATE ETCHING
### No. 1030 "CRETONNE"

THE LOTUS GLASS CO.
BARNESVILLE, OHIO

230—10 in. 2 Hld.
Crimp Bowl

223
Sugar and Cream

227—7 in.
Tall Comport

229—10 in. 2 Hld.
Salad Bowl

220—7 in.
Low Comport

231—11½ in. 2 Hld.
Sandwich

222—11 in. Hld.
Cake Tray

225—10 in.
Cheese and Cracker

224—7 in. 2 Pt.
Candy and Cover

226—5 in.
Tall Candle

228—12 in.
Console Bowl

226—5 in.
Tall Candle

221—3 Pc.
Mayonnaise Set

Plate Etching No. 1030 CRETONNE
Crystal. Lotus catalog photograph mounted on linen circa 1930-40s.
Bowl, crimped, two open handles, $34-40; sugar, $14-22; creamer, $14-22; comport tall, $24-34; salad bowl (identical to crimp bowl?), $34-40; comport, low, $14-20; plate, sandwich, two open handles, $22-30; cake tray/center handled server, $24-28; cheese and cracker, two part, $26-30; candy box w/ lid, $34-48; candle, each $24-28; console bowl, $34-46; mayo w/under plate, three piece, $36-42.
The Glass Blanks: All the items on this page are Paden City Glass line #412 Crow's Foot, square.

The LOTUS GLASS COMPANY, Barnesville, Ohio, U.S.A.
PLATE ETCHED DESIGN No. 1041

No. 75. 5½ oz.
Saucer Champagne

No. 75. 5½ oz.
Low Sherbet

No. 75. 5 oz.
Claret

No. 75. 3½ oz.
Cocktail

No. 75. ¾ oz.
Cordial

No. 75. 3½ oz.
Oyster Cocktail

No. 75. Fruit Salad

No. 75. 9 oz. Goblet

No. 73. ¾ oz.
Cordial

No. 73. 3½ oz.
Cocktail

No. 73. 5 oz.
Claret

No. 73. 5½ oz.
Low Sherbet

No. 73. 5½ oz.
Saucer Champagne

No. 73. 9 oz. Goblet

No. 73. 8 inch Plate
Also furnished in 14 inch, 10 inch and 7½ inch

No. 75. 3½ oz.
Footed Tumbler

No. 75. 7 oz.
Footed Tumbler

No. 75. 10 oz.
Footed Tumbler

No. 75. 12 oz.
Footed Iced Tea

No. 248. 15 inch R. E. Chop Plate

No. 73. 6 inch Bread and Butter Plate

No. 75. 10 oz.
Footed Tumbler

No. 73. 10 oz.
Footed Tumbler

No. 73. 12 oz.
Footed Iced Tea

Plate Etching No. 1041 VESTA PATTERN
All crystal. Lotus catalog circa 1937-38.
Goblet, flared, 9 oz., $18-24; saucer champagne, flared, 5 1/2 oz., $8-12; sherbet, low flared, 5 1/2 oz., $8-12; claret, flared, 5 oz., $8-14; cocktail, flared, 3 1/2 oz., $8-14; cordial, flared, 3/4 oz., $20-32; oyster cocktail, flared, 3 1/2 oz., $8-12; bowl, fruit salad, footed, $8-12; plate, 8", $14-18; plates (not shown), 14", $22-32, 10", $20-28, 7 1/2", $14-18; cordial, straight-sided, 3/4 oz., $20-32; cocktail, straight-sided, 3 1/2 oz., $8-14; claret, straight-sided, 5 1/2 oz., $8-14; sherbet, low, straight-sided, $8-12; saucer champagne, straight-sided, 5 1/2 oz., $8-12; goblet, straight-sided, 9 oz., $18-24; tumbler, footed, flared, 3 1/2 oz., $8-12; tumbler, footed, flared, 7 oz., $8-12 ; tumbler, footed, flared, 10 oz., $8-14; iced tea, footed, flared, 12 oz., $18-22; plate, chop, 15", $22-34; plate, bread & butter, 6", $10-14; tumbler, footed, straight-sided, 10 oz., $8-14; iced tea, footed, straight-sided, 12 oz., $18-24.
Note: Vesta was produced a long time on an almost endless variety of shapes manufactured by Duncan & Miller, Heisey, and others. The same pattern was produced with a heavy gold encrustation but no period illustrations were available for this book.

*Opposite Page:*
Plate Etching No. 1041 VESTA PATTERN continued
All crystal. Lotus catalog circa 1937-38.
Candy box, three part with lid, 6", $40-58; ash tray, cupped, 6", $18-24; ice bucket, 6", $36-48; jug, ball, 80 oz., $85-105; sugar, three-toed, $22-26; creamer, three-toed, $22-26; cigarette box, 3 pack with lid, $38-42; cigarette box, 4 pack with lid, $42-48; relish, oval, 3 part, 10", $36-44; relish, buffet, 4 section, 16", $46-58; pickle & olive, two part, 13", $20-32; celery tray, 13", $20-32.
The Glass Blanks: The round covered candy box is Fostoria Glass; the Ball Jug is Cambridge Glass #3400 line. The ice bucket appears to be a Cambridge product as well. The cream and sugar, the oval relish, buffet relish, and pickle & olive as well as the celery tray are all Heisey #1401 Empress line.

No. 91. 6 inch 3-Section
Candy Box and Cover

No. 185. 6 inch Cupped Ash Tray

No. 168. 6 inch Ice Bucket
and Handle

No. 34. 80 oz. Ball Jug

No. 175
Sugar and Cream

No. 250. 3-pack
Cigarette Box

No. 251. 4-pack
Cigarette Box

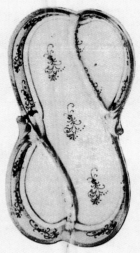

No. 244. 10 inch 3-Compartment
Oval Relish

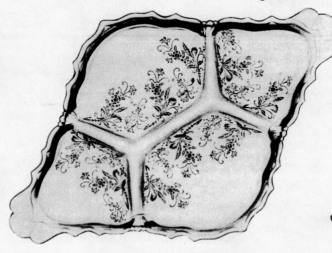

No. 242. 16 inch 4-Section Buffet Relish

No. 174. 13 inch Pickle & Olive

No. 173. 13 inch Celery Tray

No. 60. 4½ inch
Individual Coaster

No. 245. 8 inch Pretzel Stand

No. 40. 14 oz.
Handled Beer Mug

No. 205. 1 qt. Bar Bottle

No. 68. 1 qt. Shaker

No. 40. 108 oz.
Handled Beer Jug

No. 249. Combination
Coaster & Ash Tray

No. 176. Small Ash Tray

No. 871. 4½ oz.
Footed Cocktail

No. 871. 3 oz.
Taper Whiskey

No. 871. 7½ oz.
Old Fashioned Cocktail

No. 871. 8 oz.
Soda

No. 871. 10 oz.
Tall Tumbler

No. 871. 12 oz.
Tall Tumbler

No. 871. 14 oz.
Tall Tumbler

No. 243. 10 inch 7-Compartment Hors-d'œuvre

No. 232. 10½ inch Cheese and Cracker

No. 179. 7 inch Triplex Relish

Plate Etching No. 1041 VESTA Pattern continued
Crystal. Lotus original catalog circa 1937-38.
Individual coaster, $8-14; pretzel stand, $85-95; beer mug, handled, $32-40; bar bottle, 1 qt., $85-95; shaker, two part glass top, 1 qt., $95-110; jug/pitcher, handled beer (!), $95-115; coaster/sash tray, $14-18; small ash tray, $32-38; footed cocktail, $6-10; whiskey, $8-14; old fashioned, $8-12; soda tumbler, $8-12; tall tumbler, 10 oz., $10-14; tall tumbler, 12 oz., $12-16; tall tumbler, 14 oz., $14-20; hors-d'ouvre, 7 part divided, $46-58; cheese and cracker, two part, $20-32; relish, divided three part, $18-26.
The Glass Blanks: The pretzel stand is Duncan & Miller. The cocktail shaker is Heisey Glass #4225 Cobel line, and the jug is #4163 Whaley line. The small ash tray, triple relish, and 7 part tray are Heisey Empress #1401.

No. 94.  8 inch 3-Handled Vase

No. 71.  7 inch Tall Comport

: No. 172.  7 inch Oval Comport

No. 62.  8 inch Rose Bowl

No. 64.  3 pc. Mayonnaise Set
*Bowl, Plate and Ladle*

No. 240
5½ inch Semi-Tall Candle

No. 240
5½ inch Semi-Tall Candle

No. 246.  5½ inch Flared Vase

No. 241.  10½ inch Handled Cake Tray

No. 234.  9 inch 2-Handled Salad Bowl

No. 233.  11 inch 2-Handled Sandwich

Plate Etching No. 1041 VESTA PATTERN
Crystal. Lotus catalog circa 1937-38.
Vase, 3 handled, $68-76; comport, tall, $26-34; comport, tall oval, $28-38; bowl, rose, $30-36; mayonnaise w/
under plate, three piece, $24-30; candle, each $20-28; console bowl, $28-34; vase, flared, four corners, $28-34;
center handled server/cake, $22-28; bowl, two handled salad, $24-28; plate, sandwich, two handled, $22-28.
The Glass Blanks: The vase with three handles and the oval comport are Heisey Empress line #1410. The rose
bowl is Duncan Three Leaf and flared vase is Duncan's Venetian line.

No. 79 Lead Line
CRYSTAL ONLY

THE LOTUS GLASS CO., INC.
BARNESVILLE, OHIO

Deep Plate Etching
No. 1045
"Revere"

79—9 oz.
Goblet

79—5 oz.
Claret

79—3 oz.
Wine

79—¾ oz.
Cordial

79—1 oz.
Brandy

79—3½ oz.
Cocktail

79—5½ oz.
Saucer Champagne

79—Cup and
Saucer

60—8 in.
Salad Plate
(also made in
6 in. and 7 in. size)

79—Fruit Salad or Finger Bowl

79—12 oz.
Footed Ice Tea

79—9 oz.
Footed Tumbler

79—4 oz.
Footed Tumbler
or Cocktail

79—2¾ oz.
Footed Tumbler

79—5½ oz.
Low Sherbet

79—3 oz.
Sherry

79—6 oz.
Hollow Stem
Saucer Champagne

Plate Etching No. 1045 REVERE pattern
Crystal. Lotus catalog circa 1930-40s.
Goblet, $18-24; claret, $14-18; wine, $12-16; cordial, $22-32; brandy, $18-24; cocktail, $10-14; saucer champagne, $10-14; cup and saucer, $14-18; plate, salad, 8", $8-14; bowl, fruit or finger, $6-12; iced tea, $18-22; footed tumbler, 9 oz., $12-16; footed tumbler or cocktail, 4 oz., $8-12; footed tumbler, 2 3/4 oz., $8-12; low sherbet, $8-12; sherry, $14-18; hollow stem champagne, $18-24.
Note: This is the original company name as shown on Lotus catalog page. Glass author Hazel Marie Weatherman in her book *Colored Glassware of the Depression Era 2* named another etch, (Line 409) Revere. This complicates things but I strongly urge us to restore and use correct original manufacturer's names. This is the pattern that should be known as Lotus's REVERE pattern.

Plate etching 71G WILD ROSE PATTERN Crystal. 4 page Wild Rose Gold Overlay catalog dated 1953.
Relish, two part, 7 1/2", $12-18; nappy/bowl, shallow two handled, 8", $10-16; nappy, 3-toed, 7", $10-16; nappy 3-toed, 6", $10-16; plate, two handled, 9", $10-16; twin candlestick, each $12-18; sugar and cream, each $8-14; candy box with lid, 6", $14-22; relish, 3 part, two handles, 10", $14-22; mayonnaise, 3 piece, $12-22; plate, 3-toed, 7", $10-16; bowl, flared, 10", $12-16.
The Glass Blanks: Several items on this page are Viking Glass Princess line blanks, with the identifying ribbon-like base. They are the sugar and creamer, the 208 candy box, the 3 part 10" relish, the 3 piece mayo and the 10" flared bowl. The crimped nappy and 3-toed plate are Duncan's Three Leaf line.

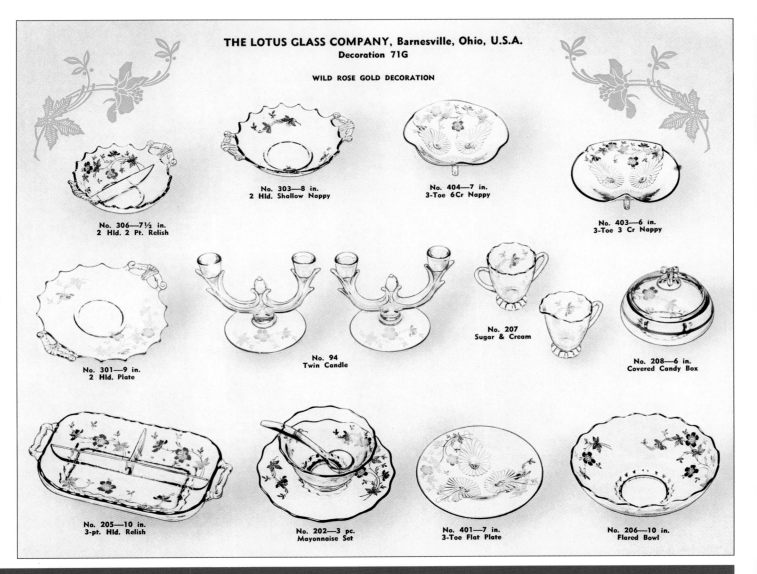

THE LOTUS GLASS COMPANY, Barnesville, Ohio, U.S.A.
Decoration 71G

WILD ROSE GOLD DECORATION

No. 306—7½ in.
2 Hld. 2 Pt. Relish

No. 303—8 in.
2 Hld. Shallow Nappy

No. 404—7 in.
3-Toe 6Cr Nappy

No. 403—6 in.
3-Toe 3 Cr Nappy

No. 301—9 in.
2 Hld. Plate

No. 94
Twin Candle

No. 207
Sugar & Cream

No. 208—6 in.
Covered Candy Box

No. 205—10 in.
3-pt. Hld. Relish

No. 202—3 pc.
Mayonnaise Set

No. 401—7 in.
3-Toe Flat Plate

No. 206—10 in.
Flared Bowl

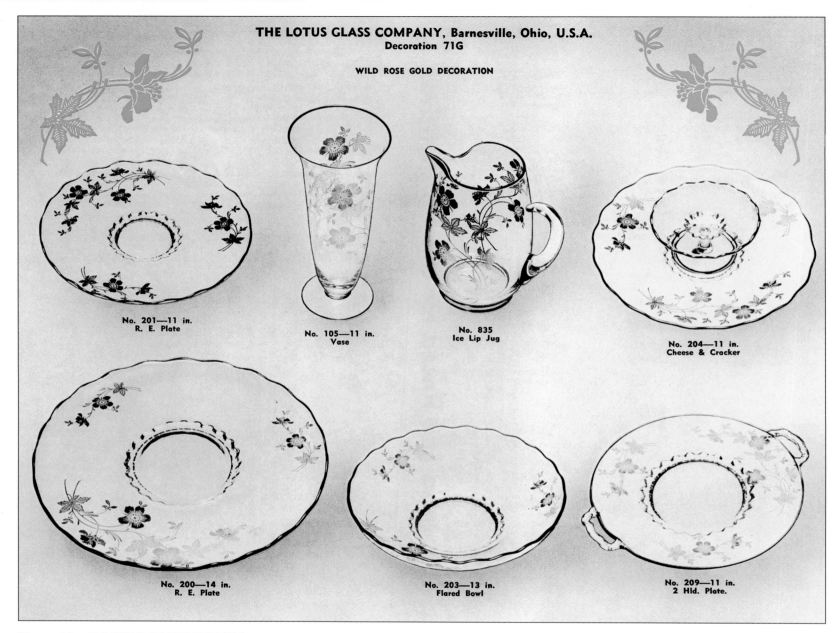

**THE LOTUS GLASS COMPANY, Barnesville, Ohio, U.S.A.**
Decoration 71G

**WILD ROSE GOLD DECORATION**

No. 201—11 in.
R. E. Plate

No. 105—11 in.
Vase

No. 835
Ice Lip Jug

No. 204—11 in.
Cheese & Cracker

No. 200—14 in.
R. E. Plate

No. 203—13 in.
Flared Bowl

No. 209—11 in.
2 Hld. Plate.

Plate etching 71G WILD ROSE PATTERN
Crystal. 4 page Wild Rose Gold Overlay catalog dated 1953.
Plate, rolled edge, 11", $14-22; vase, footed, 11", $12-18; jug, ice lip, $16-28; cheese and cracker, 2 pieces, 11",
$14-22; plate, tort rolled edge, 14", $18-32; bowl, flared, 13", $14-22; and plate, two open handles, 11", $16-20.
The Glass Blanks: All but two pieces on this page are Viking Glass blanks from the Princess line. The vase and
jug are not Viking but possibly West Virginia Glass Specialty of Weston, West Virginia.

Hand Made       Hand Decorated

*Gold Decorators Since 1912*

# No. 71 G. Wild Rose Gold Overlay

### 22 Karat Gold

Produced only by Lotus craftsmen with whom quality gold has been a tradition, decorating on the lovely shapes and finest blanks. Makes a combination of practical gift items at a price that your most exacting price conscious customer will appreciate.

## Styled and Priced for this Competitive
## 1953 Market
## WILD ROSE

Gold Overlay Furnished in the Following List of Items

| NO. | | RETAIL PRICE EACH | NO. | | RETAIL PRICE EACH |
|---|---|---|---|---|---|
| 200—14 in. R. E. Plate | | $10.00 | 94— | Twin Candle | $10.00 |
| 201—11 in. R. E. Plate | | 8.50 | 105—11 | in. Vase | 7.50 |
| 202— | 3-pc. Mayonnaise Set | 8.50 | 835— | Ice Lip Jug | 8.50 |
| 203—13 in. Flared Bowl | | 10.00 | 401— 7 | in. 3-Toe Flat Plate | 4.50 |
| 204—11 in. Cheese & Cracker | | 10.00 | 403— 6 | in. 3-Toe 3-Cr Nappy | 4.50 |
| 205—10 in. 3-pt. Hld. Relish | | 8.50 | 404— 7 | in. 3-Toe 6-Cr Nappy | 4.50 |
| 206—10 in. Flared Bowl | | 8.50 | 303— 8 | in. 2Hld. Shallow Nappy | 4.50 |
| 207— | Sugar & Cream | 7.50 | 301— 9 | in. 2Hld. Plate | 4.50 |
| 208— 6 in. Covered Candy Box | | 7.50 | 306—7½ | in. 2Hld. 2-pt. Relish | 4.50 |
| 209—11 in. 2 Hld. Plate | | 8.50 | (Less Discount) | | |

Plus Package Charge

*Compare the Quality and Price and You Will Be Convinced*

### THE LOTUS GLASS CO., INC. • Barnesville, Ohio, U.S.A.

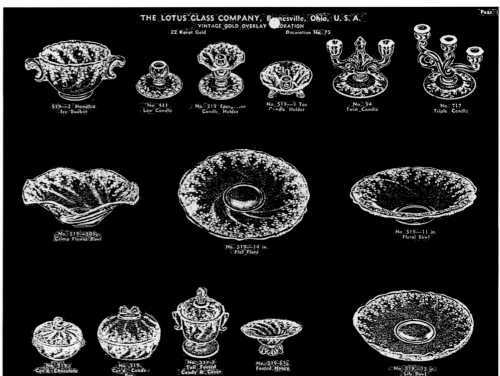

Plate etching 75 called both VINATGE GOLD OVERLAY
Crystal. Created page from Lotus catalog pages circa 1940-50s.

Handled ice bucket, $85-100; candle, low, each $22-30; candle holder, epergnes, each $36-46; candle holder, three-toed, each $36-42; twin candle, each $42-50; triple candleholder, each $60-68; bowl, crimp flower, $28-38; plate, torte, 14", $34-38; bowl, flared, 11", $28-38; box, covered chocolate, $78-85; box, covered candy, $80-95; jar, tall-footed candy with lid, $125-150; dish, honey, footed, $24-32; bowl, lily, 13", $32-38.

The Glass Blanks: The ice bucket and all three bowl in the middle row as well as the four images of the covered candy boxes and the honey dish are all Heisey #1519 Waverly line blanks. The 3-toed candle is Heisey #1401 Empress, the twin candle is Heisey #124 Trident and the triple stick is Heisey #142 Cascade line.

Note: This page is a composite I created of two pages from a very illegible catalog. Three pages of this pattern were found, illustrated largely on Heisey blanks. As shown here, the bottom left four items are all cut from a second page and overlay some poorer quality images on the original page shown here. The quality of this image and the need to alter the original pages is regretted, but to show some of this pattern it was deemed important. This pattern is similar to, but not the same as, Roseate shown later in this chapter.

Plate etching 71G WILD ROSE PATTERN continued
Plate etching 71G WILD ROSE PATTERN
Crystal. 4 page Wild Rose Gold Overlay catalog dated 1953.
Cover for Lotus catalog brochure promoting Wild Rose Gold Overlay decorations. Note this is dated 1953 and includes the then current list of available pieces.

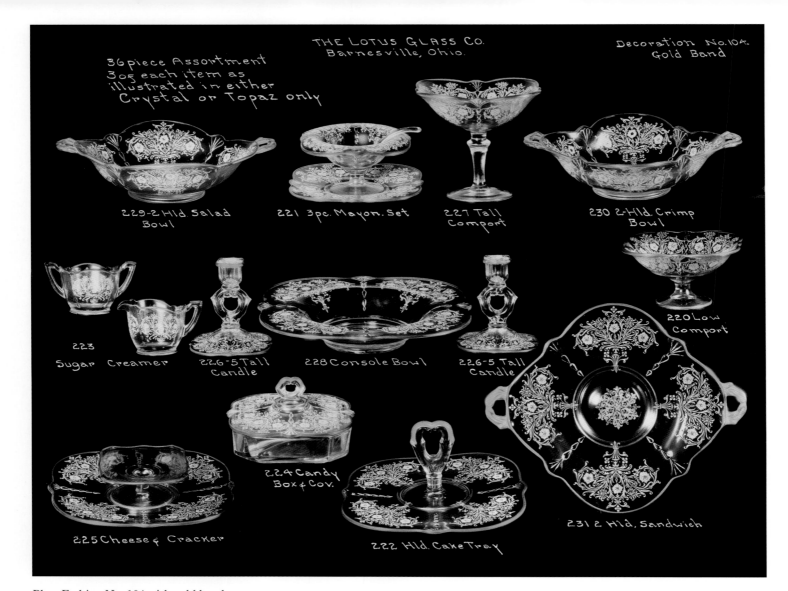

Plate Etching No. 104 with gold band

Crystal or Topaz as shown. Lotus catalog page circa 1930-40s. All prices are for crystal; for topaz add 30-40% more.

Bowl, salad, handled, $30-38; Mayonnaise set, 3 piece, $28-34; comport, tall, $38-44; bowl, crimped handled (uncertain how to distinguish between this and the salad bowl first appearing on this page), $30-38; sugar, $16-22; creamer, $16-22; candle, 5", each $28-34; bowl, console, $34-46; comport, low, $20-28; cheese and cracker, two piece, $30-38; candy box, divided with lid, $30-34; tray, cake, center handled, $28-34; sandwich tray, two handled, $28-34.

The Glass Blanks: All of the glass blanks used for this decoration shown here are Paden City Glass square Crow's Foot line #412.

## 24 STEMWARE LINE

# Decoration No. 109

*Crystal Bowl with Rose Stem and Foot
also Green Stem and Foot*

| NO. | OZ. | | | DOZ. |
|---|---|---|---|---|
| 24 | —9 | Goblet . . . Optic | $ | 6.00 |
| 24 | —5½ | High Sherbet Optic | | 6.00 |
| 24 | —5 | Low Sherbet Optic | | 6.00 |
| 24 | —3½ | Oyster Ckt'l. Optic | | 6.00 |
| 24 | —2 | Wines . . . Optic | | 5.90 |
| 24 | —3½ | Cocktail . . Optic | | 5.90 |
| 24 | —12 | Ice Tea, Ftd. Optic | | 6.00 |
| 24 | —10 | Ftd. Tumbler Optic | | 6.00 |
| 24 | —7 | Ftd. Tumbler Optic | | 6.00 |
| 24 | —2¾ | Ftd. Tumbler Optic | | 5.90 |
| 24 | —3 pt. | Jug . . . . . Optic | | 24.00 |
| 24 | —1 qt. | Decanter . . Optic | | 21.00 |
| 60 | —6 in. | B. & B. Plate . . . | | 7.20 |
| 60 | —7½ in. | Salad Plate . . . . | | 7.80 |
| 60 | —8 in. | Salad Plate . . . . | | 9.00 |
| 60 | —10 in. | Service Plate . . . . | | 16.20 |
| 60 | —12 in. | Service Plate . . . . | | 22.20 |

Plate Etching No. 109 with gold band
Crystal with green or rose stem and feet. Lotus promotional brochure circa 1930s.
The 9 oz. goblet is the only item shown, $46-54.
The Glass Blanks: The stem is Central Glass stem #2007 known as the Kimberly line when undecorated. Central closed in 1939 so this and other uses of Central Glass blanks all predate 1940.
Note: The *Pottery, Glass & Brass Salesman* of March 29, 1928, illustrates this pattern and claims, "This is one of the newest creations, the gracefully shaped crystal bowl is adorned with a unique deep plate etching." See the following illustration for more detailed pricing on other pieces.

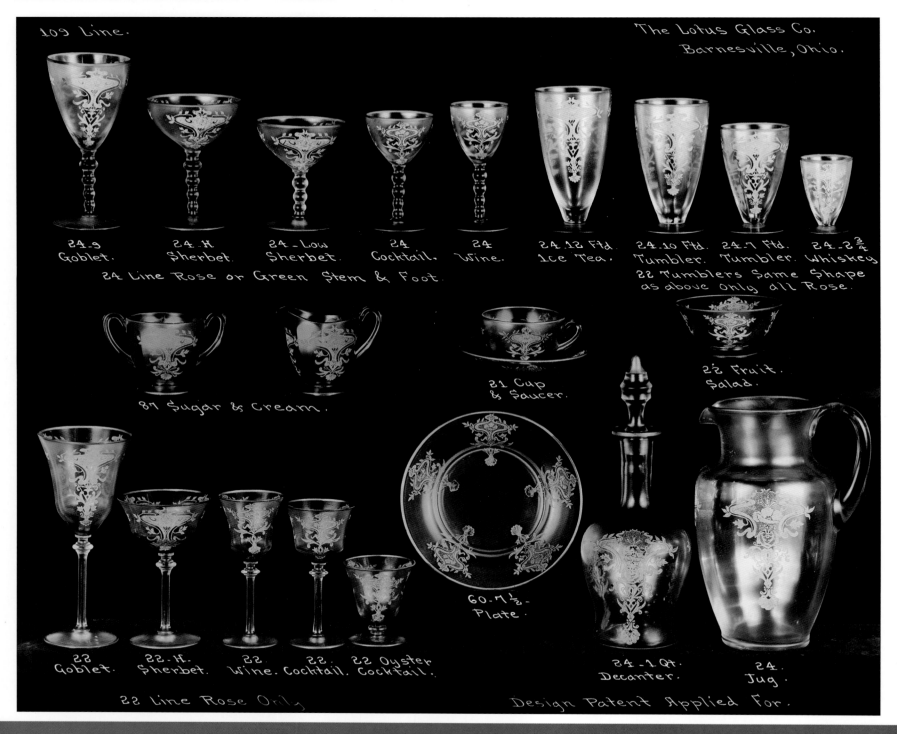

109 Line.

The Lotus Glass Co.
Barnesville, Ohio.

24.9
Goblet.

24.H.
Sherbet.

24-Low
Sherbet.

24
Cocktail.

24
Wine.

24.12 Ftd.
Ice Tea.

24.10 Ftd.
Tumbler.

24.7 Ftd.
Tumbler.

24-2¾
Whiskey

24 Line Rose or Green Stem & Foot.

22 Tumblers Same Shape
as above Only all Rose.

87 Sugar & Cream.

31 Cup
& Saucer.

2½ Fruit.
Salad.

22
Goblet.

22.H.
Sherbet.

22
Wine.

22.
Cocktail.

22 Oyster
Cocktail.

60-7½-
Plate.

24-1 Qt.
Decanter.

24.
Jug.

22 Line Rose Only

Design Patent Applied For.

Plate Etching No. 110 RAMBLER ROSE with gold decoration & No. 118 MINTON with gold decoration. Crystal. Lotus loose catalog sheet. Circa 1950-60s. Rambler Rose plate, luncheon, $20-28; goblet, $24-30; cocktail, $16-20; iced tea, footed, $22-28; sherbet/saucer champagne, $22-26; Minton goblet, $24-30; cocktail, $16-20; plate, luncheon, $20-28; sherbet/saucer champagne, $22-26; iced tea, footed, $22-28.
Note: Rambler Rose and Minton were produced by Lotus to compliment existing so-named and exceedingly popular china patterns. Other glass companies also made both decorations and used the same names, although minor differences in the glass shapes may exist. The prices for these patterns are driven not completely by their status as collectibles, but by their replacement values. These patterns remain as popular today for formal tableware as they were in the 1940-60s.

*Opposite Page:*
Plate Etching No. 109 with gold band
Crystal with rose or green feet or tumblers, all rose, for line #24, line #22 all rose only. Lotus catalog page illustrating two lines of stemware for this one decoration.
Line 24 goblet, 9 oz., $46-54; sherbet/saucer champagne, tall, $16-24; sherbet, low, $16-24; cocktail, $20-24; wine, $20-26; iced tea, footed, $30-36; tumbler, footed, 10 oz., $20-28; tumbler, footed, 7 oz., $20-28; whiskey, 2 3/4 oz., $22-30; sugar, $20-24; creamer, $20-24; cup and saucer set, $34-38; bowl, fruit salad, $14-20; all Line 22 stemware goblet, $38-45; sherbet, saucer champagne, high, $16-24; wine, $20-26; cocktail, $20-26; oyster cocktail, $18-22; plate, 7 1/2", $14-20; decanter with stopper, 1 qt., $145-165; jug/pitcher, $100-125.
The Glass Blanks: All of the blanks on this page are Central Glass Company products, except perhaps the jug/pitcher. It appears to be a Weston Glass product/shape. Stemware line 24 is Central's Kimberly stem line #2007. The footed tumblers are Central's #1447; the cup and saucer is line #2005. The line number for the 22 stemware line is unknown. The decanter is Central #503.

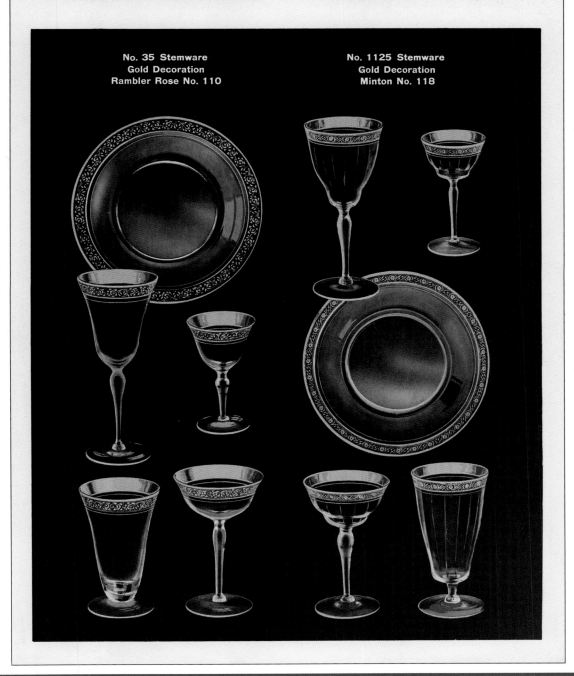

THE LOTUS GLASS COMPANY . . . BARNESVILLE OHIO, U.S.A.

No. 35 Stemware
Gold Decoration
Rambler Rose No. 110

No. 1125 Stemware
Gold Decoration
Minton No. 118

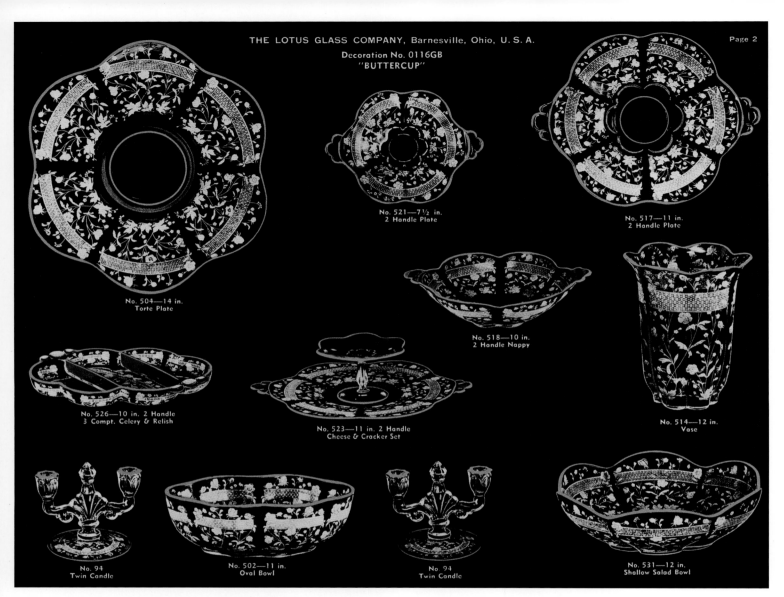

No. 521—7 1/2 in.
2 Handle Plate

No. 517—11 in.
2 Handle Plate

No. 504—14 in.
Torte Plate

No. 518—10 in.
2 Handle Nappy

No. 514—12 in.
Vase

No. 526—10 in. 2 Handle
3 Compt. Celery & Relish

No. 523—11 in. 2 Handle
Cheese & Cracker Set

No. 94
Twin Candle

No. 502—11 in.
Oval Bowl

No. 94
Twin Candle

No. 531—12 in.
Shallow Salad Bowl

Plate etching 116GB (0116B) BUTTERCUP Pattern.
Crystal. Lotus catalog page circa 1940-50s.
Plate, torte, 14", $30-36; plate, two handled, 7 1/2", $12-20; plate, two handled, 11", $26-34; relish & celery, 3 part, 10", $28-38; cheese and cracker, two part, 11", $28-36; nappy/bowl, 10", $30-36; vase, 12", $34-42; twin candle, each $48-58; bowl, oval, 11", $36-44; bowl, shallow salad, 12", $34-40.
The Glass Blanks: All of the pieces on this page are on Duncan & Miller Glass's Canterbury line blanks, except the candlesticks which are Heisey Trident sticks.
Note: Stemware was produced by Lotus to match this pattern and the pattern was produced both with and without the gold trim.

*Opposite Page:*
Plate Etching No. 118 with gold IMPROVED MINTON Crystal. Lotus catalog page dated to pre-1924 by the use of the name Lotus Cut Glass Co.; the company name changed, deleting the word "Cut," in 1924.
Jelly, low, 4 1/2 oz., $6-10; jelly, high, 4 1/2 oz., $8-12; goblet, $12-16; sherbet, high, $8-12; sherbet, low, $6-10; tumbler, iced tea, 12 oz., $4-8; tumbler, 10 oz., $3-6; cheese and cracker, two part, $12-18; café parfait, $6-10; wine, $6-10; cocktail, $5-8; plate, cake, center handled, $10-16; finger bowl and under plate, 6", $8-12; plate, salad, 8", $6-10.

Gold Encrustation No. 118
Improved Minton.

Low Jelly.
Dec. 118.
25 - 4 1/2.

High Jelly.
Dec. 118.
25 - 4 1/2.

Goblet
Dec. 118.
25.

High Sherbet
Dec. 118.
25

Low Sherbet
Dec. 118.
25

Ice Tea Tumbler.
Dec. 118
740 - 12 oz.

Tumbler - 740 - 10 oz.
Dec. 118

1801 - 10 "
Cheese & Cracker
Dec. 118.

Cafe
Parfait
Dec. 118.
25.

Wine
Dec. 118
25.

Cocktail
Dec. 118.
25.

Cake Plate
Dec. 118.
1802 - 10 1/2 Hdl.

25 - Finger Bowl
25 - 6 "  "  Plate
Dec. 118.

Salad Plate
Dec. 118.
59 - 8 "

Lotus Cut Glass Co. Barnesville, Ohio.

GOLD ENCRUSTATION 118B MINTON
LOTUS GLASS COMPANY, BARNESVILLE, OHIO.

23 LOW FTD. SHERBET    106 GRAPE JUICE JUG    23 - 3½ OZ. COCKTAIL    23 GOBLET    105 - 3 PT. JUG OPT. 118 B.    23 HIGH SHERBET
OPTIC 118B.            OPTIC 118 B              OPTIC 118 B          OPTIC 118 B                                OPTIC 118B.

840 - 5 OZ. TUMBLER

23 - 2½ OZ. WINE
OPTIC 118B

840 - 10 OZ. TUMBLER    8 - 3 PT. COV. JUG                87 - 4 PT. JUG  OPTIC 118 B.        840 - 12 OZ. ICE TEA    109 ICE TEA JUG.
OPTIC 118 B.           OPTIC 118 B                                                           OPTIC 118 B.          OPTIC 118 B

Plate Etching No. 118B with gold MINTON
Crystal. Lotus hand-colored photograph mounted on linen after 1924.
Sherbet, low, $12-16; jug, grape juice with lid, $28-40; cocktail, 3 1/2 oz., $10-14;
goblet, $16-24; jug, 3 pint, $32-44; sherbet, high, $12-18; tumbler, 5 oz., $4-7; tumbler,
10 oz., $4-8; jug, bulbous with lid, 3 pint, $36-48; jug, belled, 4 pint, $40-52; wine, 2 1/
2 oz., $12-20; tumbler, iced tea, 12 oz., $6-10; jug, iced tea with lid, $34-46.
Note: The line number 118B refers to the two thin gold "bands" running above and
below the usual Minton etched and gold encrusted decoration.

No 90 Minton Encrusted.
Stemware
Decoration No. 122
22 Karat Gold

Gold Decoration No.196 Amethyst.

200-10" Cheese & Cracker    200-10" Comport.    200-10" Hld. Cake Plate.

200-5"          200-9"          200-10"          200-9"          200-7"
Low Comport.    Candlestick.    Bowl & Base.     Candlestick.    Tall Comport

The Lotus Glass Co. Barnesville, Ohio.

Plate Etching No. 122 with gold MINTON encrustation No. 90
Crystal. Lotus partial catalog sheet circa 1940-50s. Plate, $20-28; cocktail, $18-24; sherbet/saucer champagne, $20-28; iced tea, footed, $20-28; goblet, $26-32.
The Glass Blanks: The stems are Central Glass Winslow stemware line, but the catalog style suggests this is from the era when Central moulds had been acquired by Imperial. Imperial Glass acquired them circa 1940.

Plate Etching No. 196 with gold
Amethyst. Lotus catalog page circa 1930s.
Cheese & cracker, two part, $45-55; comport, 10", $48-54; cake plate, center handled, 10", $38-42; comport, low, 5", $38-44; candlestick, 9", each $45-50; bowl, 10", fruit and black base, $80-86; comport, tall, 7", $42-48.
The Glass Blanks: this page shows items on Central Glass blanks. The cheese and cracker is their #1003, the 10" comport is line #200, the center handled server is Central's #1435, and the candlestick and bowl are Central, but the line number is unknown. As all items are amethyst on the page, it would stand to reason the smaller comports are also Central and similar forms are known from Central.

Decoration No. 792.    No. 55 Stemware Line    The Lotus Glass Co. Inc.
All Crystal Optic or    Barnesville, Ohio.
Crystal Stem & Foot with
Rose Bowl.

55 - 12 oz.    55 - 9 oz.    55 - 6 oz.    55 - 2½ oz.    55 - 3½ oz    55 - 2½ oz.    55 - ¾ oz.
Ftd. Ice Tea    Ftd. Tumbler    Ftd. Tumbler    Ftd. Tumbler    Cocktail.    Wine.    Cordial.

55    60 - 7½ in.    55 - 5½ oz.    55 - 5½ oz.    21 - Cup & Saucer
Ftd. Fruit Salad    Salad Plate.    High Sherbet    Low Sherbet

21 - 1 Qt. Decanter.    60 - 9 in. Dinner Plate.    55 - 9 oz. Goblet.    24 - 48 oz. Jug.

Plate Etching No. 792 with gold
Crystal. Lotus catalog photograph mounted on linen. Circa 1930s. Cited as available in crystal stem and foot with
rose/pink, which would be 30-50% more.
Iced tea, footed, 12 oz., $20-28; tumbler, footed, 9 oz., $12-18; tumbler, footed, 6 oz., $10-14; tumbler, footed, 2 1/2
oz., $20-24; cocktail, 3 1/2 oz., $10-14; wine, 2 1/2 oz., $20-24; cordial, $38-42; fruit salad, footed, $8-12; plate,
salad, 7 1/2", $10-16; sherbet, high, 5 1/2 oz., $10-12; sherbet, low, 5 1/2 oz., $10-12; cup & saucer, $26-34; decanter,
1 qt. with stopper, $75-90; plate, dinner, 9", $26-32; goblet, 9 oz., $28-34; jug, 48 oz., $60-80.
Note: The footed tumblers are all Central line #144 and the stems are Central #1455. The decanter is Central's
#530 with the jeweled stopper. The jug appears to be Weston Glass.

*Opposite Page:*
Plate Etching No. 792 with gold
Crystal, pink or green. Lotus
catalog photograph mounted on
linen. Circa 1930s. Pieces appear
to be available in any of pink,
green or crystal. Pink and green
prices could be 30-50% more.
The prices suggested are for the
piece as shown.
Vase, 3-footed, tall, 9", $60-78;
tray, pastry, center handled, 12",
$24-35; comport, tall, 7", $36-46;
candlestick, 3 1/2", each $18-24;
bowl, flared console, 13", $38-48;
relish (candy), three part with
lid, 6", $38-46; celery tray, 11",
$24-32; whipped cream/
mayonnaise set, three pieces,
$26-36.
The Glass Blanks: The tall
compote, 7", on the first row, is
Central's #2005. The console set
on the second row is Central
Glass #2000, the relish/candy
with cover is Central's #2005 (a
flatter, plainer finial than the
similar Fostoria box of similar
design), the celery and whipped
cream/mayo set are Central's
#2001 or #2002 line. The 3-
footed vase is Duncan's #12.

Decoration 792.

The Lotus Glass Co.
Barnesville, Ohio.

204 - 9 in. Tall Vase.
3 Ftd.

201 - 12 in. Hld.
Pastry.

201 - 7 in.
Tall Comport.

201 - 13 in. Flared.
Bowl.

201 - 3½ in.
Low Candle.

201 - 6 in. 3 Sect.
Covered Relish.

201 - 11 in. 2 Hld.
Celery Tray.

200 - 3 Pc.
Whipped Cream Set.

Decoration 792.

The Lotus Glass Co.
Barnesville, Ohio.

205-12½ in.
6 Toe Flared Bowl.

204-4 in. 2 Hld.
Ice Tub Oblong.

206-12½ in.
Flared Bowl.

204-5½ in.
Tall Candle.

204-12½ in. Fld. Fruit
Bowl. Decoration 790.

200-10 in.
Cheese Cracker.

201-11 in. 2 Hld.
Sandwich. Dec. 791.

200-10 in.
Hld. Cake.

*Opposite Page:*

Plate Etching No. 792 with gold. Crystal, pink or green. Lotus catalog photograph mounted on linen. Circa 1930s. Pieces appear to be available in any of the colors pink, green or crystal. Pink and green prices would be 30-50% more than crystal. The prices suggested are for the piece as shown.

Bowl, flared, 6 toe, 12 1/2", $58-68; ice tub, two handled oblong, $55-70; bowl, flared, 12 1/2", $34-38; candle, tall, 5 1/2", each $50-65; bowl, footed fruit, 12 1/2", decoration 790, $80-94; cheese and cracker, 10", two part, $32-40; plate, sandwich, two handled, 11", decoration 791, $38-46; tray, cake, center handled, 10", $32-44.

Notes: The page includes decoration 792, with examples of 790 (shown on the fruit bowl) different from 792 in that the gold is no longer just on the etched rim but follows the etching pattern down into the vessel. It is the same etching, different gold application. Etching 791 is shown on the bottom on the two handled sandwich tray. Decoration 791 is different from 792 in that the gold is solid as it covers the etching at the border and 792 has two bands of gold around part of the etching. Both are shown here. The Glass Blanks: The six toe bowl on the first row is Central Glass blank #2014; the ice bucket is Central's and was part of line #2002 and #2001. The tall candlesticks are #2020 from Central and the bowl is Central's #2025. The cheese and cracker set is Central #1103, the two handled platter is #2001, and the center handled tray is an unknown Central line number.

Decoration 792.

The Lotus Glass Co. Barnesville Ohio.

206 - 8 3/4 in. Rose Bowl.

202 - 12 in. Flat. Rim Vase 3 Ftd.

207 - Large Ftd. Flared Vase.

203 - 5 1/2 Semi Tall Candlestick.

203 - 12 in. Ftd. Crimp Bowl.

201 - 12 1/2 in. Oblong Platter.

Sugar & Creamer.

201 - 11 in. Oblong Bowl.

Plate Etching No. 792 with gold, continued.

Crystal, pink or green. Lotus catalog page circa 1930. Pieces appear to be available in pink, green or crystal. Pink and green prices would be 30-50% more. The prices suggested are for the pieces in the colors shown.

Rose Bowl, 8 3/4", $56-64; Vase, 3-footed, flat rim, 12", $46-52; vase, footed, flared, $70-78; candlestick, "semi" tall candlestick, 5 1/2", each $30-38; bowl, three-footed crimped, 12", $50-58; platter, oblong, 12 1/2", $60-68; creamer, $22-28; sugar, $22-28; bowl, oblong, 11", $58-64.

The Glass Blanks: The footed, flared vase #207 at the end of the first row has been attributed to Central, but neither this author or Central expert Tim Schmidt has found verification to date. The platter and bowl on the bottom row are Central's #2002 and the cream and sugar are unknown Central line numbers. The 3-footed vase is Duncan's #12 and the "semi" tall candle is Duncan's #28, and the footed, crimped bowl is Duncan Three Leaf line. The Rose Bowl is Duncan's #8 bowl.

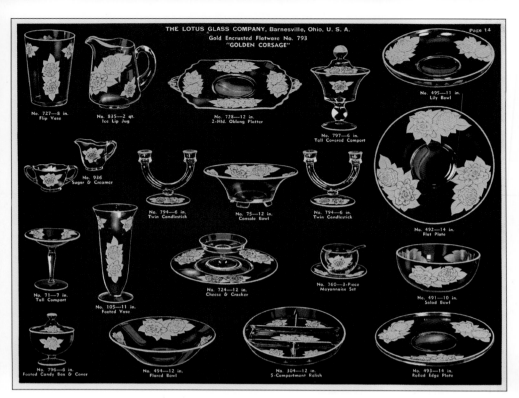

THE LOTUS GLASS COMPANY, Barnesville, Ohio, U.S.A.
Gold Encrusted Flatware No. 793
"GOLDEN CORSAGE"

Page 14

No. 727—8 in. Flip Vase
No. 835—2 qt. Ice Lip Jug
No. 728—12 in. 2-Hld. Oblong Platter
No. 797—6 in. Tall Covered Comport
No. 495—11 in. Lily Bowl
No. 936 Sugar & Creamer
No. 794—6 in. Twin Candlestick
No. 75—12 in. Console Bowl
No. 794—6 in. Twin Candlestick
No. 492—14 in. Flat Plate
No. 71—7 in. Tall Comport
No. 105—11 in. Footed Vase
No. 724—12 in. Cheese & Cracker
No. 760—3-Piece Mayonnaise Set
No. 491—10 in. Salad Bowl
No. 796—6 in. Footed Candy Box & Cover
No. 494—12 in. Flared Bowl
No. 304—12 in. 5-Compartment Relish
No. 493—14 in. Rolled Edge Plate

Plate Etching No. 793 with gold GOLD COURSAGE Pattern. Crystal. Lotus catalog page circa 1940s.
Vase, flip, 8", $16-22; jug, with ice lip, 2 qt., $18-28; platter, two handled, 12", $16-24; comport, with lid, 6", $22-32; bowl, lily, 11", $20-28; sugar, $12-18; creamer, $12-18; candlestick, twin, 6", $20-26; bowl, console, 4-toed, 12", $12-22; plate, flat torte, 14", $18-26; comport, tall, 7", $18-24; vase, footed, 11", $14-26 cheese and cracker, 12", two part, $16-22; mayonnaise set, three pieces, $18-24; bowl, salad, 10", $20-26; candy box, footed with lid, 6", $16-24; bowl, flared, 12", $14-24; relish, 5 part divided, 12", $22-28; plate, rolled edge, 14", $18-26.
The Glass Blanks: The No. 797 comport is Paden City Glass of Paden (pay-din) City, West Virginia.

Plate etched decoration No. 796 with gold. Crystal, pink, green, amber or black available. Lotus catalog photograph, hand-colored and mounted on linen. Circa 1930-40s. Pink and green prices would be 30-50% more than crystal. Black pieces would be 50-80% more than crystal. Amber and crystal would be priced similarly. The prices suggested are for the pieces as shown.
Compote, tall, $42-54; vase, three-toed, $85-105; candle stick, tall, each $30-40; bowl, crimped, three-toed, $30-45; bowl, cupped, three-toed, $40-55; candy box with cover (divided?), $58-68; candlestick, low, each $18-24; console bowl, six-footed, $20-28; tray, center handled cake or sandwich, $22-36; bowl, flared rim, $50-68; plate, cake, two open handles, $24-32; cheese and cracker, two part, $32-40; bowl, console, rolled rim, $22-38; mayonnaise three part set, $34-40; bowl, salad, two open handles, $24-32.
The Glass Blanks: The three-toed black vase is Duncan as are the three pieces with three feet. The candlestick is Duncan's #28. The covered candy is Central's #2500.

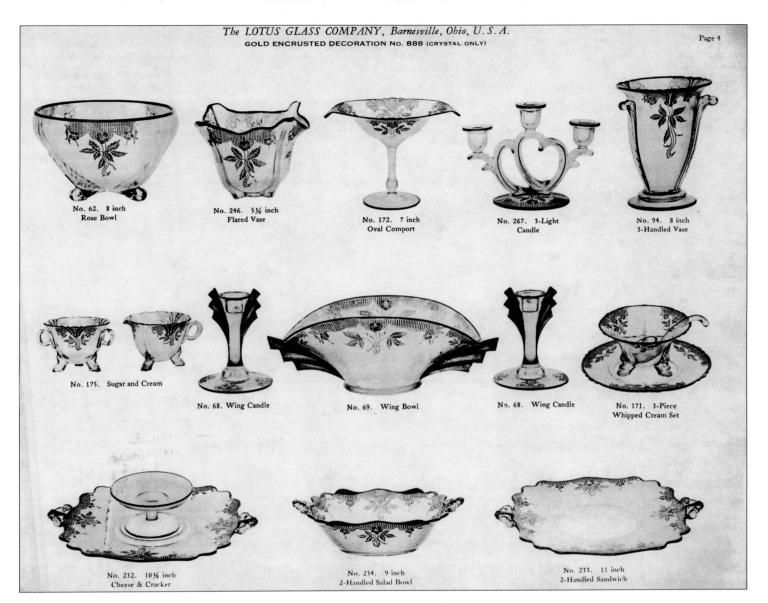

No. 62.   8 inch
Rose Bowl

No. 246.   5½ inch
Flared Vase

No. 172.   7 inch
Oval Comport

No. 267.   3-Light
Candle

No. 94.   8 inch
3-Handled Vase

No. 175.   Sugar and Cream

No. 68.   Wing Candle

No. 69.   Wing Bowl

No. 68.   Wing Candle

No. 171.   3-Piece
Whipped Cream Set

No. 232.   10½ inch
Cheese & Cracker

No. 234.   9 inch
2-Handled Salad Bowl

No. 233.   11 inch
2-Handled Sandwich

Plate etched decoration No. 888 with gold
Crystal. Lotus catalog page, 1937-38.
Rose bowl, 8", $14-26; vase, flared, 5 1/2", $20-30; compote, oval, 7", $22-32; candle, 3-light, each $45-58; vase, 3 handled, 8", $35-48; sugar, three-toed, $16-24; creamer, three-toed, $16-24; candle, wing, each $30-35; bowl, wing, $40-50; whipped cream set/mayonnaise 3 piece set, $38-42; cheese and cracker, two part set, $28-38; bowl, salad, two handled, 9", $28-34; plate, sandwich, two handled, 11", $ 22-32.
The Glass Blanks: The wing candle stick is Duncan & Miller's No. 16 line, as is the bowl. The rose bowl is Duncan's three leaf and flared vase is their Venetian line. The oval comport, 3 handled vase, sugar, creamer, and 3 part whipped cream are all Heisey #1401 Empress line. The three light candle stick is Imperial Glass No. 753.

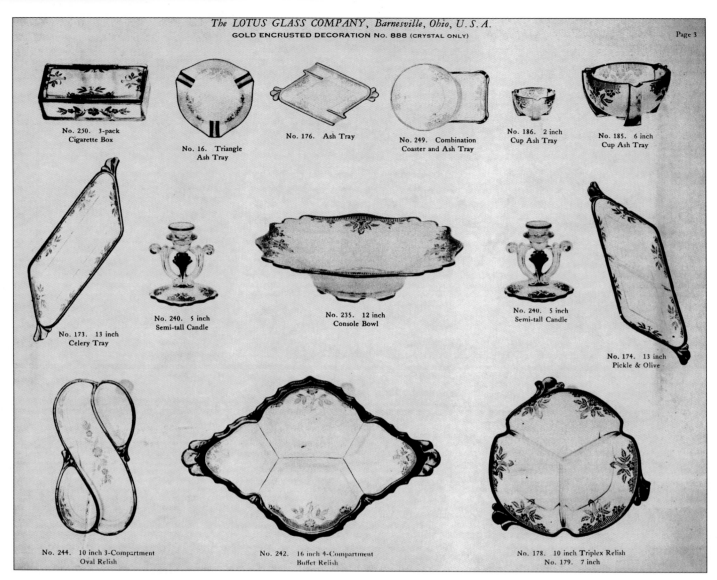

No. 250. 3-pack
Cigarette Box

No. 16. Triangle
Ash Tray

No. 176. Ash Tray

No. 249. Combination
Coaster and Ash Tray

No. 186. 2 inch
Cup Ash Tray

No. 185. 6 inch
Cup Ash Tray

No. 173. 13 inch
Celery Tray

No. 240. 5 inch
Semi-tall Candle

No. 235. 12 inch
Console Bowl

No. 240. 5 inch
Semi-tall Candle

No. 174. 13 inch
Pickle & Olive

No. 244. 10 inch 3-Compartment
Oval Relish

No. 242. 16 inch 4-Compartment
Buffet Relish

No. 178. 10 inch Triplex Relish
No. 179. 7 inch

Plate etched decoration No. 888 with gold
Crystal. Lotus catalog page, 1937-38.
Cigarette box, 3-pack, $28-38; ash tray, triangle, $4-8; ash tray, diamond, $10-16; combination ash tray and coaster, $12-18; ash tray, cup, 2", $12-16; ash tray, cup, 6", $10-16; celery tray, 13", $22-32; candlestick, semi-tall, 5", each $30-36; bowl, console, 12", $35-45; pickle and relish tray, 13", two part, $24-34; relish, oval 3 part, 10", $24-32; relish, buffet, 4 part, 16", $34-42; relish, 3 part, 10", $22-30 and 7", $24-32.
The Glass Blanks: The diamond-shaped ash tray, 13" celery, 12" pickle & olive, 3 compartment relish, 4 part buffet relish, and 7" & 10" relishes are all Heisey Empress line #1401. The two cup-form ash trays are Duncan's No. 11 & 12 ashtrays, the triangle ash tray is also Duncan, and Lotus uses the Duncan number, #16. The candlesticks are Central glass.

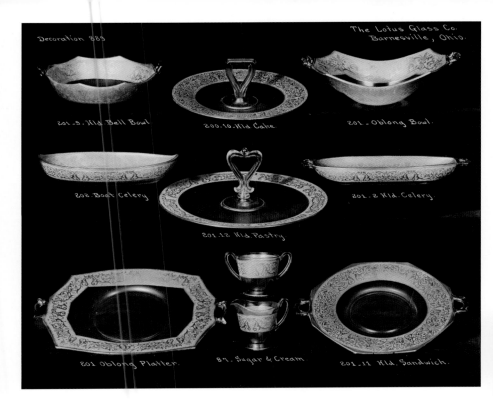

Plate etched decoration 889 with gold
Pink or green. Lotus catalog photograph, hand-colored and linen mounted, circa 1930s. The prices suggested are for the pieces as shown, but little difference exists between green and pink prices.
Bowl, bell, two handled, 9", $36-44; tray, cake, center handled, 10", $32-38; bowl, oblong two open handles, $45-50; celery boat, $36-42; tray, center handled pastry, 12", $38-46; celery, two handles open, $38-42; platter, oblong two open handles, $45-55; sugar, $18-24; creamer, $18-24; plate, sandwich, two open handles, 11", $32-38.
Note: Plate etching 889 appears to have been immensely popular for Lotus. It appears with the wide, acid etched band encrusted in gold, with thin gold bands on either side of the etched band and on a number of different shapes and stem lines, only some of which appear on the following pages.
The Glass Blanks: The bell bowl is the Central #2002 line, the center handled tray on the top row is Central #1435; the top row oblong bowl is Central's #2002; the second row— far right two handled celery is Central's with an unknown line number. The bottom row features all Central Glass blanks with the oblong platter being #2002, the sugar and cream are unknown line numbers, and the far right handled sandwich is line #2001.

Plate etched decoration 889 with gold continued
Pink or green. Lotus catalog photograph, hand-colored and linen mounted, circa 1930s. The prices suggested are for the pieces as shown, but little difference exists between green and pink prices.
Bowl, footed, $46-52; rose bowl, $44-50; bowl, rolled edge, $46-52; candlestick, tall, each $30-38; bowl, three-toed, crimped, $46-52; bowl, rolled edge, three-toed, $44-48; muffin, handled, 10 1/2", $28-38; bowl, flared, three-footed, $46-50.
The Glass Blanks: The bottom row, center piece, the handled muffin, appears to be Central's #2001 line. The tall candlestick is Duncan's #28, the four pieces with 3 toes are Duncan's Three Leaf line, and the two #206 bowls are Duncan's #8 bowl.

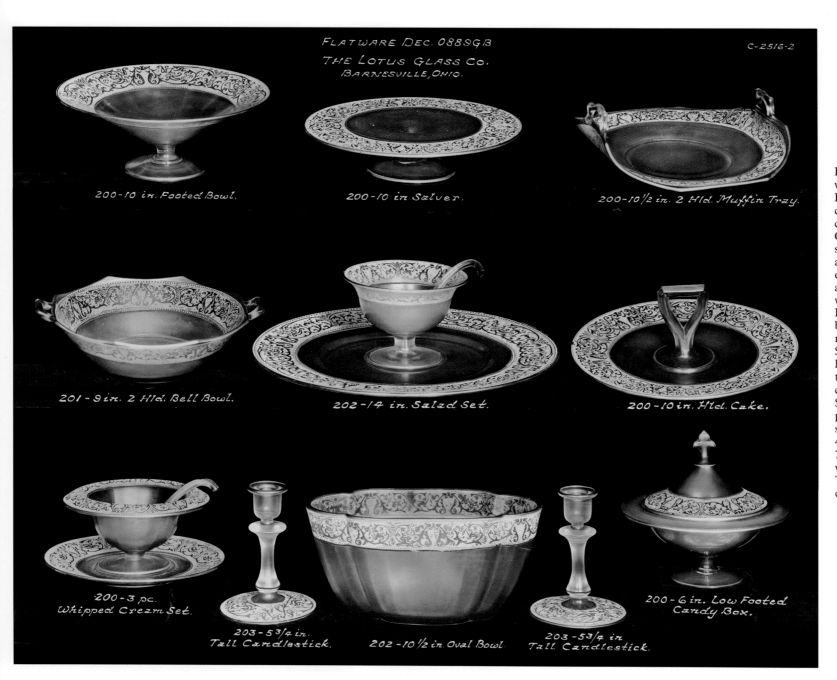

FLATWARE DEC. 0889GB
THE LOTUS GLASS CO.
BARNESVILLE, OHIO.

C-2516-2

200-10 in. Footed Bowl.

200-10 in Salver.

200-10½ in. 2 Hld. Muffin Tray.

201-9 in. 2 Hld. Bell Bowl.

202-14 in. Salad Set.

200-10 in. Hld. Cake.

200-3 pc.
Whipped Cream Set.

203-5¾ in.
Tall Candlestick.

202-10½ in. Oval Bowl.

203-5¾ in.
Tall Candlestick.

200-6 in. Low Footed
Candy Box.

Plate etched decoration 889 with gold.
Pink, green or amber. Lotus catalog photograph, hand-colored and linen mounted. Circa 1930s. The prices suggested are for the pieces as shown, but little difference exists between green and pink prices. Amber would be 50% less.
Bowl, footed, 10", $38-44; bowl/salver, 10", $30-36; tray, muffin, two handled, 10 1/2", $28-38; Bowl, bell, two handled, $28-44; salad set, three piece, 14", $55-65; tray, cake, center handled, 10", $32-40; whipped cream 3 piece set, $45-55; candlestick, tall, 5 3/4", each $36-44; bowl, oval, 10 1/2", $65-75; candy box, low-footed with lid, 6", $50-60.
The Glass Blanks: The tall candlestick is Duncan's #28.

Plate etched decoration 889 with gold continued.

Pink, green or amber. Lotus catalog photograph, hand-colored and linen mounted, circa 1930s. The prices suggested are for the pieces as shown, but no difference exists between green and pink prices. Amber would be 50% less. Whip cream/mayonnaise set, 3 piece, $30-40; comport, tall, 7", $28-36; bowl, nut, center handled, 10", $34-42; candle, low, each $18-22; bowl, console, flared/rolled edge, 13", $36-46; relish/candy box with lid, $26-36; ice tub, two handled, $54-62; cheese and cracker set, two piece, 10", $26-34. Notes: There are several Central Glass blanks used on this page, they include: the whip cream is line #2000 or 2001; the compote is line # 2005; the second row candlesticks and console bowl are #2000 line; the candy/relish is #2005; the ice tub is line #2000; and the cheese and cracker is #1003. Central closed in 1939, so this page pre-dates that time.

Dec. 889.

The Lotus Glass Co,
Barnesville, Ohio.

200. Whip
Cream Set.

201.7
Tall Comport.

201-10 Hld.
Nut Bowl.

201-3 1/2
Low Candle.

201-13
Fld. Bowl.

201-3 1/2
Low Candle.

201.6
Cov'd. Relish.

201.4
Hld. Ice Tub.

200.10.
Cheese & Cracker.

C-2516.

FLATWARE DEC. 0889GB.
THE LOTUS GLASS CO.
BARNESVILLE, OHIO.

201-6 in. 3 Sec. Cov'd.
Relish.

201-11 in. 2 Hld. Sandwich
Plate.

200-1 lb.
Candy Jar.

200-10 in. Cheese & Cracker

201-3 1/2 in.
Low Candlestick.

201-13 in. Flared Bowl.

201-3 1/2 in.
Low Candlestick.

202-4 in.
Low Candlestick.

202-11 in.
Oval Boat Bowl.

202-4 in.
Low Candlestick

201-10 in. Handled
Nut Bowl.

201-4 in. Ice Tea Tub.

200-10 in. Rolled Edge Bowl.

201-10 in. Lily Bowl.

201-7 T. Comport

Plate etched decoration 889 with gold continued Pink, green, crystal or amber. Lotus catalog photograph, hand-colored and mounted on linen, circa 1930s. The prices suggested are for the pieces as shown, but little difference exists between green and pink prices. Amber or crystal would be 50% less than pink or green.

Relish/candy box, 3 part divided with cover, 6", $30-42; Plate, sandwich/cake, two open handles, 11", $18-28; candy jar, footed with lid, $42-52; cheese & cracker, two part, 10", $18-24; candlestick, low, 3 1/2", each $22-30; bowl, flared and rolled rim, 13", $58-68; candlestick, low, 4", each $22-30; bowl, oval boat, 11", $58-68; "Iced tea tub" or ice tub, 4", $45-55; bowl, rolled edge, 10", $40-46; bowl, nut, center handled, 10", $38-42; bowl, lily, 10", $42-50; compote, tall, 7", $18-28. The Glass Blanks: The covered relish/candy is Central Glass.

No. 78 Gold Band Stemware
Decoration No. 0889
22 Karat Gold

Plate etch decoration No. 0889 with gold Crystal. Partial Lotus catalog page, circa 1950-60s. Shown here is the popular acid etching 889 (the same as 0889). This illustrates the decoration on stem line No. 78. It is from an original catalog page, cropped to present only the partial page with 889 here; other panels of this page are shown elsewhere in their respective decorations/patterns. Sherbet/saucer champagne, $10-16; cocktail, $8-14; plate, $16-22; goblet, $18-24; footed tumbler/iced tea, $14-20.

*Lotus*

*Lotus*

## Decoration No. 889

### 21 STEMWARE LINE

*Crystal Bowl and Rose Stem and Foot*
*also Green Stem and Foot*

| NO. | OZ. | | | DOZ. |
|---|---|---|---|---|
| 21 | 9 | Goblet . . . | Optic | $13.80 |
| 21 | 5½ | High Sherbet | Optic | 13.80 |
| 21 | 5½ | Low Sherbet | Optic | 13.80 |
| 21 | 5 | Parfait . . . | Optic | 13.80 |
| 21 | 3 | Wine . . . . | Optic | 13.70 |
| 21 | 3½ | Cocktail . . | Optic | 13.70 |
| 21 | | Fruit Salad . | Optic | 15.00 |
| 21 | 12 | Ftd. Ice Tea . | Optic | 13.80 |
| 21 | 9 | Ftd. Tumbler | Optic | 13.80 |
| 21 | 6 | Ftd. Tumbler | Optic | 13.70 |
| 21 | 2½ | Ftd. Tumbler | Optic | 13.70 |
| 21 | 48 | Ftd. Jug . . | Optic | 48.00 |
| 60 | 7½in. | Salad Plate . . . . | | 16.80 |
| 60 | 8 in. | Salad Plate . . . . | | 18.00 |
| 60 | 12 in. | Salad Plate . . . . | | 42.00 |

Plate etch decoration No. 889 on stemware line No. 21. Rose/pink and crystal as well as green and crystal. Lotus promotional brochure, circa 1920-30s. There is little difference in price for pink or green.
The goblet only, as illustrated, 9 oz., $24-32.
From the literature shown here, we find a list of other pieces produced but not shown.

Plate etch decoration 899-02
Crystal. Lotus catalog photograph mounted on linen. Circa 1920-30s.
Cheese and cracker, two part, 10", $20-30; salad set/mayonnaise 3 pieces, $22-32; candlestick, each $18-24; bowl, bulb, 7 3/4" with black base, $35-45; plate, handled cake/center handled server, 10", $18-26; plate/salver, 10", $18-24.

Plate etch No. 900
Crystal. Lotus catalog photograph mounted on linen. Circa 1920-30s.
Bowl, six-toed, 12 1/2", $25-35; comport, tall, $25-35 ; plate, handled cake/center handled server, $30-38; bowl, three-toed, three crimp, $36-44; bowl, center handled nut, $30-38; candle, low, 3 1/2", each $20-24; bowl, console, flared, 13", $38-38; bowl, two handled bell, $28-36; muffin, two handled, $28-34; plate, sandwich, two handled, 11", $28-34; relish/candy with cover, 3 part, $38-46; cheese and cracker, 2 part, 10", $34-38.
The Glass Blanks: All of the forms on this page are from Central Glass except the 203 crimped bowl. The three-toed bowl is #2014; the tall comport #2005; the handled nut bowl is line #1435; the sticks are from the #200 line, as is the console bowl. Bell bowl is line #3003; the Muffin and handled sandwich are #2001; the covered candy is #2005; and the cheese and cracker #1435. The crimped bowl is the Duncan Three Leaf line.
Note: See decoration #901, as it is the same etch with less gold encrustation. The two patterns/decorations would go together well. A stemware line matching this pattern is called Goldenrod. Perhaps that name should apply to these pieces as well?

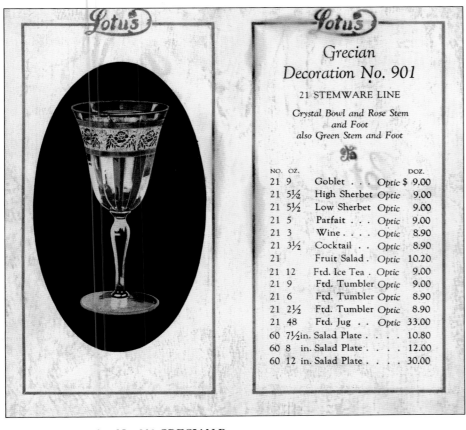

## Grecian
### Decoration No. 901

21 STEMWARE LINE

*Crystal Bowl and Rose Stem
and Foot
also Green Stem and Foot*

| NO. | OZ. | | | DOZ. |
|-----|-----|------|------|------|
| 21 | 9 | Goblet . . . Optic | $ | 9.00 |
| 21 | 5½ | High Sherbet | Optic | 9.00 |
| 21 | 5½ | Low Sherbet | Optic | 9.00 |
| 21 | 5 | Parfait . . . | Optic | 9.00 |
| 21 | 3 | Wine . . . . | Optic | 8.90 |
| 21 | 3½ | Cocktail . . | Optic | 8.90 |
| 21 | | Fruit Salad . | Optic | 10.20 |
| 21 | 12 | Ftd. Ice Tea . | Optic | 9.00 |
| 21 | 9 | Ftd. Tumbler | Optic | 9.00 |
| 21 | 6 | Ftd. Tumbler | Optic | 8.90 |
| 21 | 2½ | Ftd. Tumbler | Optic | 8.90 |
| 21 | 48 | Ftd. Jug . . | Optic | 33.00 |
| 60 | 7½ in. | Salad Plate . . . . | | 10.80 |
| 60 | 8 in. | Salad Plate . . . . | | 12.00 |
| 60 | 12 in. | Salad Plate . . . . | | 30.00 |

Plate etch decoration No. 901 GRECIAN Pattern.
Crystal bowl with rose/pink stem and foot or crystal with green stem and foot. Lotus promotional brochure, circa 1920-30s. Prices are similar for either color combination.
The goblet only, as shown, 9 oz., $28-38.
From the literature's listing featured here we learn the other shapes produced.
Note: See decoration #900, as it is the same etch, except all of the etched area is heavily gold encrusted. The two patterns/decorations would go together well.

Plate etch decoration No. 902
Pink or green. Lotus catalog photograph hand-colored and mounted on linen, circa 1930s. Prices are similar for either pink or green.
Bowl, handled nut, 10", $38-46; relish/candy with lid, 3 part divided, 6", $50-58; plate, cake, center handled server, 10", $34-42; whipped cream set, 3 piece, $45-55; salad set, three pieces, 14", $54-64; candy box, low, footed with lid, 6", $50-54; bowl, footed, 10", $38-44; comport, tall, 7", $38-42; ice tub, two tab handles, 4", $58-66.
The Glass Blanks: All pieces are Central Glass except the low footed candy box. The center handled nut appears to be line #1435; the 3 part candy is #2005; the center handled cake is #1435; the whipped cream/mayo is probably #2001; the salad set is #1103. The footed bowl on the bottom row is line #2000; the tall comport is #2005; and the ice tub is again line #2001. Recall that Central closed in 1939.

Decoration 902.

The Lotus Glass Co.
Barnesville, Ohio.

206. R.E. Bowl.

206. Rose Bowl.

206 Fld. Bowl.

201. 2. Hld. Celery Tray.

201. 12. Hld. Pastry.

202. Boat Celery.

201. Oblong Bowl.

87 Sugar & Cream.
Design Patent 77484.

201 Oblong Platter.

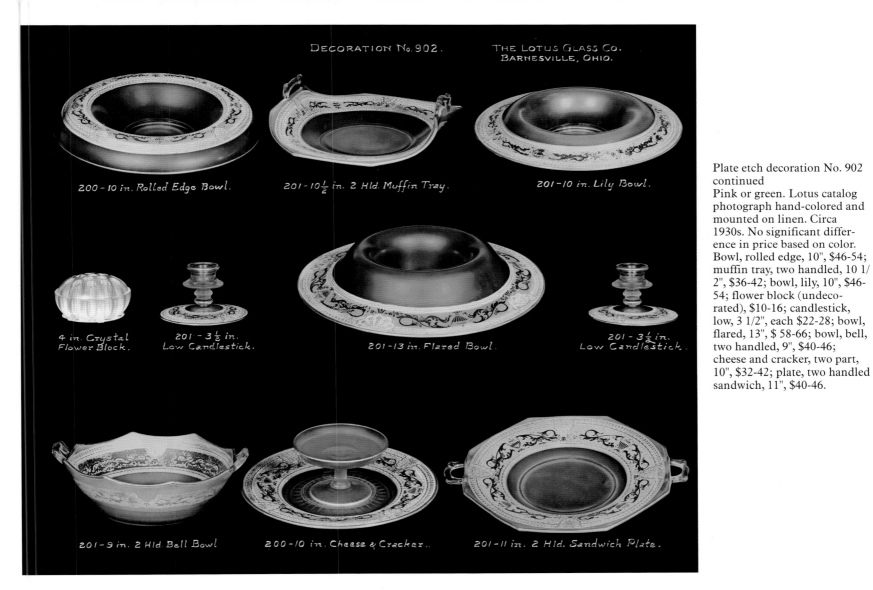

DECORATION No. 902.

THE LOTUS GLASS CO.
BARNESVILLE, OHIO.

200 - 10 in. Rolled Edge Bowl.

201 - 10½ in. 2 Hld. Muffin Tray.

201 - 10 in. Lily Bowl.

4 in. Crystal Flower Block.

201 - 3½ in. Low Candlestick.

201 - 13 in. Flared Bowl.

201 - 3½ in. Low Candlestick.

201 - 9 in. 2 Hld. Bell Bowl

200 - 10 in. Cheese & Cracker.

201 - 11 in. 2 Hld. Sandwich Plate.

Plate etch decoration No. 902 continued
Pink or green. Lotus catalog photograph hand-colored and mounted on linen. Circa 1930s. No significant difference in price based on color. Bowl, rolled edge, 10", $46-54; muffin tray, two handled, 10 1/2", $36-42; bowl, lily, 10", $46-54; flower block (undecorated), $10-16; candlestick, low, 3 1/2", each $22-28; bowl, flared, 13", $ 58-66; bowl, bell, two handled, 9", $40-46; cheese and cracker, two part, 10", $32-42; plate, two handled sandwich, 11", $40-46.

*Opposite Page:*
Plate etch decoration No. 902 continued.
Pink or green. Lotus catalog photograph hand-colored and mounted on linen, circa 1930s. Prices are similar for either pink or green, amber is about 50% less. Prices suggested are for the pieces as shown.
Bowl, rolled edge, $50-58; bowl, rose, $52-60; bowl, footed, $35-45; celery tray, two handled, $45-50; plate, pastry/cake, center handled server, 12", $34-42; celery boat, $28-34; bowl, oblong, $58-64; sugar and cream, each $22-24; platter, oblong, $58-64.
The Glass Blanks: The celery tray, oblong bowl, and platter are Central Glass products line 2001 and 2002. The two bowls numbered 206 are Duncan's #8 bowl.

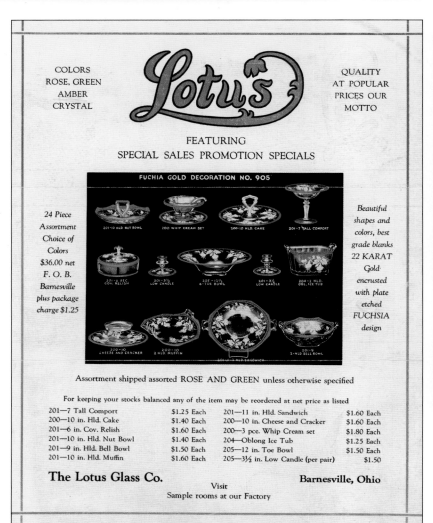

Plate etch decoration No 905 (same as 0905) FUCHSIA pattern
Crystal, as shown, also reported in rose/pink, green, and amber. Lotus three fold promotional brochure, circa 1930s. Prices are for crystal. Amber would be not be substantially different in price. Green or pink would be approximately 40-60% more for this decoration.
Bowl, center handled nut, $22-32; whip cream/mayonnaise set, 3 pieces, $18-26; plate, cake, center handled server, 10", $22-32; comport, tall, $22-34; relish/candy with lid, 3 part divided, $28-36; candle, low, 3 1/2", each $20-26; bowl, six-toed, $32-42; ice tub, oblong, two handled, $36-46; cheese and cracker, two part, $26-32; muffin, two handled, 10", $18-28; plate, sandwich, two open handles, $22-32; bowl, two handled bell, 9", $20-32.
Note: This same etch appears without gold, yet bears the same number. See the No Gold chapter for additional illustrations.

Plate etch decoration No. 908, stemware line 18, LA FURISTE Pattern
Crystal, pink or green. Lotus catalog photograph hand-colored and mounted on linen, circa 1920-30s. Priced as shown. Pink and green are 40-60% more than crystal, adjust for color accordingly.
Goblet, $45-55 (crystal); sherbet, high/saucer champagne, $38-46; sherbet, low, $28-38; cocktail, $20-28 (crystal); wine, $45-55; cordial, $55-65 (crystal); ice tea, footed, 12 oz., $34-42; tumbler, footed, 10 oz., $28-34; tumbler, footed, 6 oz., $28-34; tumbler, whiskey-footed, 2 1/2 oz., $45-55; cup and saucer, $55-65; bowl, fruit salad, footed, $20-26 (crystal); goblet with gold gilding, add ten to twenty dollars above a not gilded price ($45-55); goblet, $58-68; plate, salad, $20-26; decanter, $190-210; jug, $160-180.
Note: La Furiste was featured in *The Pottery, Glass & Brass Salesman* of July 1920 when it was touted as a "new thing."
The Glass Blanks: The stemware is Morgantown, the decanter is Central Glass #530, the cup and saucer their #2005 line, and the jug appears to be Weston Glass.

Plate etch decoration No. 908, stemware line 18, LA FURISTE Pattern continued Crystal, pink or green. Lotus catalog photograph hand-colored and mounted on linen. Circa 1920-30s. Priced as shown. Pink and green are 40-60% more than crystal; adjust for color accordingly.

Bowl, rolled edge, 10", $55-65 (crystal); muffin, two handled, 10 1/2", $52-64; bowl, center handled nut, 10", $75-85; celery, two handled, $46-54; celery boat, $40-48; candle, low, 3 1/2", each $38-46; bowl, console, flared, 13", $76-86; bowl, two handled bell, 9", $45-55 (crystal); cheese and cracker, two part, 10", $55-65; plate, cake, two handled, 11", $48-58 (crystal).

Note: La Furiste was featured in *The Pottery, Glass & Brass Salesman* of July 1920 when it was touted as a "new thing." The Glass Blanks: The open handled muffin, bowl, and plate appear to be Central Glass, as does the low candle.

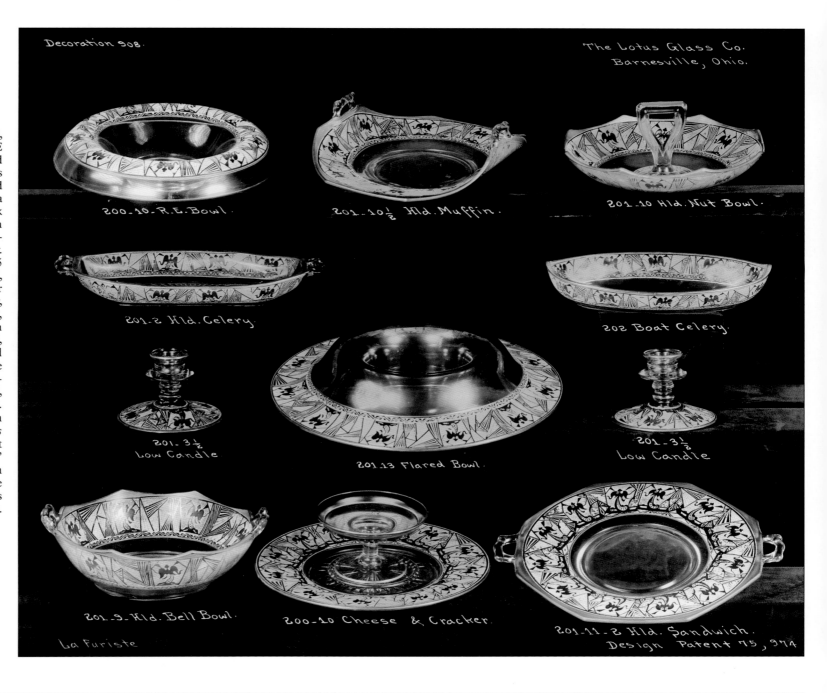

Decoration 908.

The Lotus Glass Co. Barnesville, Ohio.

200-10-R.E. Bowl.

201-10½ Hld. Muffin.

201-10 Hld. Nut Bowl.

201-2 Hld. Celery.

202 Boat Celery.

201-3½ Low Candle

201-13 Flared Bowl.

201-3½ Low Candle

201-9-Hld. Bell Bowl.

200-10 Cheese & Cracker.

201-11-2 Hld. Sandwich. Design Patent 75,974

La Furiste

Plate etch decoration No. 908, stemware line 18, LA FURISTE Pattern
Pink or green. Lotus catalog photograph hand-colored and mounted on linen. Priced as shown.
Bowl, flared, three-footed, $68-78; bowl, rose, three-footed, $68-78; bowl, rolled edge, three-footed, $60-74; candle, tall, 5 1/2", each $40-55; bowl, three crimps, three-footed, $60-74; platter, oblong, open handles, $60-74; sugar and cream, each $26-36; bowl, oblong, open handles, $60-74.
Note: While crystal is not shown, it likely exists in these forms. La Furiste was featured in *The Pottery, Glass & Brass Salesman* of July 1920 when it was touted as a "new thing."
The Glass Blanks: The bottom row is all Central Glass, the platter is line #2002, the cream and sugar lines numbers are not known, and the oblong bowl is the same mold as the platter, only cupped while the glass was yet hot. The tall candlestick is Duncan & Miller #28 and the three pieces, each being three-footed, are Duncan's Three Leaf line.

Plate etch decoration No. 908, stemware line 18, LA FURISTE Pattern
Crystal, pink or green. Lotus catalog photograph hand-colored and mounted on linen. Circa 1920-30s. Priced as shown. Pink and green are 40-60% more than crystal, adjust for color accordingly.
Bowl, flared, $64-72; rose bowl, $70-78; bowl, rolled edge, $64-76; relish/candy with cover, 3 part divided, 6", $76-84; plate, pastry/cake, center handled serving, 12", $48-58 (crystal); comport, tall, 7", $68-76; ice tub, two open handles, $76-84; whip cream set/mayonnaise, 3 piece, $66-74; plate, cake, center handled serving, 10", $70-78.
Note: La Furiste was featured in *The Pottery, Glass & Brass Salesman* of July 1920 when it was touted as a "new thing."
The Glass Blanks: The covered relish/candy is Central Glass. All three bowls across the top row are forms of Duncan's #8 bowl.

## Decoration No. 908
## (La Furiste)
### STEMWARE LINE

Modern Trend Design
(Design Patent Applied For)

*Gold Band on Inner and Outer Edge
of Plate—Etched Border—22 Karat
Furnished in Rose, Green and Crystal*

| NO. | | PER DOZ. |
|---|---|---|
| 18—9 oz. Goblet . . . (optic) | | $ 7.80 |
| 18—6½oz. High Sherbet | " | 7.80 |
| 18—6½oz. Low Sherbet | " | 7.80 |
| 18—3½oz. Cocktail . . . | " | 7.70 |
| 18—2¾oz. Wine . . . . . | " | 7.70 |
| 18—1½oz. Cordial. . . . | " | 7.70 |
| 18— Fruit Salad | " | 9.00 |
| 21—12 oz. Ftd. Ice Tea | " | 7.80 |
| 21—9 oz. Ftd. Tumbler | " | 7.80 |
| 21—6 oz. Ftd. Tumbler | " | 7.70 |
| 21—2½oz. Ftd. Tumbler | " | 7.70 |
| 18—4 pt. Jug. . . . . . | " | 27.00 |
| 18—1 qt. Decanter. . . | " | 27.00 |
| 21— Cup & Saucer . . . | | 14.40 |
| 60—6 in. Bread & Butter Plate | | 7.20 |
| 60—7½in. Salad Plate . . . . . | | 7.80 |
| 60—8 in. Salad Plate . . . . . | | 9.00 |
| 60—10 in. Service Plate . . . . | | 16.20 |
| 60—12 in. Service Plate . . . . | | 24.00 |

## Decoration No. 908
## (La Furiste)

Modern Trend Design
(Design Patent Applied For)

*Gold Band on Inner and Outer Edge
of Plate—Etched Border—22 Karat*

*Furnished in Rose, Green and Crystal*

| NO. | | PER DOZ. |
|---|---|---|
| 200—10 in. Handled Cake. . . . | | $18.00 |
| 200—10 in. Cheese & Cracker . . | | 18.00 |
| 200—10 in. Rolled Edge Bowl . . | | 18.00 |
| 201—13 in. Flared Bowl . . . . . | | 24.00 |
| 201—3½ in. Low Candlestick . . . | | 9.00 |
| 201—10 in. Hld. Nut Bowl . . . . | | 18.00 |
| 201—4 in. Hld. Ice Tub . . . . | | 18.00 |
| 201—7 in. Tall Comport . . . . . | | 18.00 |
| 201—6 in. 3 Sec. Covered Relish | | 18.00 |
| 201—11 in. 2 Hld. Sandwich Plate | | 18.00 |
| 201—10 in. 2 Hld. Muffin . . . . | | 18.00 |
| 201—9 in. 2 Hld. Bell Bowl . . | | 18.00 |
| 200— 3 Pc. Whipped Cream | | 18.00 |
| 202—10½in. Oval Bowl . . . . . . | | 24.00 |
| 203—5¼ in. Tall Candlestick . . . | | 12.00 |

Plate etch decoration No. 908, stemware line 18, LA FURISTE Pattern continued
Original Lotus brochure listing pieces made in the line and their prices.

MARTHA GOLD ENCRUSTATION 1003 GE.
THE LOTUS GLASS COMPANY, BARNESVILLE, OHIO.

520 CORDIAL OPTIC

740-10 OZ. TUMBLER OPTIC

520 COCKTAIL OPTIC

350-7" LOW-COMPORT OPT.

740-12 OZ. HLD. ICE TEA OPTIC

520-2½ OZ. WINE OPTIC

740-2½ OZ. WISKEY OPTIC

520 LOW SHERBET OPTIC

488 BRIDGE SET

25 CAFE PARFAIT OPTIC

350 GRAPE FRUIT OPTIC

740-12 ICE TEA OPT.

740-5 OZ. TUMBLER OPTIC

520 HIGH SHERBET OPTIC

60-8" SALAD PLATE

520-9 OZ. GOBLET OPTIC

740-10 OZ. TUMBLER OPTIC

97-4 PT. JUT' OPTIC

60 GUEST ROOM SET OPTIC

25 FINGER BOWL & PLATE OPT.

57-½ lb. CANDY JAR OPTIC

Plate etch decoration No 1003 MARTHA
Pattern continued
Original Lotus brochure listing pieces made
in the line and their original prices.

520 Goblet Opt.
1003 G E

*Opposite Page:*
Plate etch decoration No. 1003
MARTHA pattern
Crystal. Lotus catalog photograph,
circa 1920-30s.
Cordial, $30-40; tumbler, 10 oz.,
$10-14; cocktail, $10-12; comport,
low, 7", $20-28; ice tea, 12 oz.,
handled, $20-28; wine, 2 1/2 oz.,
$20-22; tumbler, whiskey, 2 1/2 oz.,
$20-28; bridge set, three pieces,
$75-85; sherbet, low, $8-10; café
parfait, $8-10; grapefruit, $14-22;
ice tea, 11 oz., $14-20; tumbler, 5
oz., $10-16; sherbet, high/saucer
champagne, $8-14; goblet, 9 oz.,
$24-32; tumbler, 10 oz., $10-14;
jug, 4 pint, $42-54; guest room set/
tumbler up, two part, $48-58;
finger bowl and under plate, $18-
24; plate, salad, 8", $12-16; candy,
footed with lid, 1/2 lb., $36-44.

## Martha Plate Etching 1003 Gold Enc.

| | | Doz. |
|---|---|---|
| 97-2 | Grape Juice Jug | $33.00 |
| 8-3 | Covered Ice Tea Jug | 54.00 |
| 97-4 | Jug | 36.00 |
| 740-2½ | Whiskey | 12.00 |
| 740-5 | Grape Juice Tumbler | 12.00 |
| 740-10 | Table Tumbler | 13.20 |
| 740-12 | Ice Tea Tumbler | 13.20 |
| 740-12 | Hld. Ice Tea Tblr. | 14.40 |
| 520-9 | Goblet | 14.00 |
| 520-5½ | High Sherbet | 14.00 |
| 520-5½ | Low Sherbet | 14.00 |
| 25-6 | Cafe Parfait | 13.20 |
| 520-3½ | Cocktail | 13.20 |
| 520-2½ | Wine | 12.00 |
| 520-¾ | Cordial | 11.40 |
| 350 | Grape Fruit | 24.00 |
| 57-½ | Candy Jar | 24.00 |
| 60-12 | Service Plate | 36.00 |
| 60-8 | Salad Plate | 21.00 |
| 60-6 | Bread & Butter Plate | 15.00 |
| 488-3pc | Boudoir Set (Oval Tray, Glass, Jug) | 48.00 |
| 50-1 | Decanter | 42.00 |
| 58 | Sugar & Cream | 30.00 |
| 60 | Guest Room Set | 18.00 |
| 350-7 | Low Comport | 42.00 |
| 25 | Finger Bowl | 16.00 |
| 25-6 | Finger Bowl Plate | 16.00 |
| 350-7 | Salad Bowl | 36.00 |
| 350-6 | Tall Comport | 31.80 |

## Mary Louise Gold Encrustation

### PLATE ETCHING NO. 1008

*Diamond Optic*

| NO. | OZ. | | DOZ. |
|---|---|---|---|
| 357 | 10 | Goblet . . . . . | $15.00 |
| 357 | 6½ | High Sherbet . . | 15.00 |
| 357 | 6½ | Low Sherbet . . | 15.00 |
| 357 | 5 | Parfait . . . . . | 15.00 |
| 357 | 2½ | Wine . . . . . . | 14.40 |
| 357 | 4 | Cocktail . . . . | 14.40 |
| 357 | 4½ | Oyster Cocktail. | 14.40 |
| 357 | 12 | Ftd. Ice Tea . . . | 15.00 |
| 357 | 8½ | Ftd. Tumbler . . | 14.40 |
| 357 | 3 | Ftd. Whiskey . . | 13.80 |
| 357 | | Ftd. Finger Bowl | 16.20 |
| 357 | | Ftd. Jug . . . . . | 48.00 |
| 60 | 8 in. | Salad Plate . . . | 18.00 |
| 60 | 7½ in. | Salad Plate . . . | 16.80 |
| 60 | 6 in. | Bread and Butter Plate | 15.00 |

*No. 357 Goblet*

Plate etch decoration No. 1008 MARY LOUISE GOLD ENCRUSTATION Pattern
Crystal only. Original Lotus brochure listing pieces made in the line and their prices.
Goblet, 10 oz., $40-48.
The Glass Blanks: Heisey Glass King Arthur line #3357.

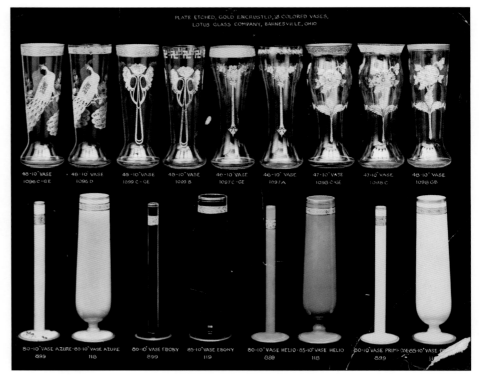

Plate etch decorations of various numbers
Crystal and opaque colors. Lotus catalog photograph hand-colored and mounted on linen.
Circa 1930s.
Peacock etched vases, $28-45; vase, art deco poppy, $20-28; same vase with swastika, $30-48; 1097C with gold, $18-24, without gold, $14-18; any of the three poppy vases, $18-32.
azure vase, stick, $58-70; #118, $60-80; ebony vase, stick, $80-95; #118, $85-105; helio vase, stick, $55-68; #118, $65-80; primrose vase, stick, $50-68; #118, $60-78.
The Glass Blanks: The opaque bottom row is all Cambridge Glass Company, using their original company color names.

# Gold BROCADE
# Silver BROCADE
## by Lotus

# Georgian Gold

A Lotus creation of sparkling, brilliant American made Crystal encrusted with 22 karat burnished paste gold. All the stemware items are handblown full lead crystal. This exclusive Lotus process of gold encrusting is also applied to the matched serving pieces as illustrated below. For the hostess who wants the best in table appointments American Beauty Georgian Gold by Lotus is the answer.

1971—6x5 ½ in.
Covd. Candy

8" x 8" Square
12" x 12" Square
14" x 14" Square (not shown)

8 in. Circle
12 in. Circle
14 in. Circle (not shown)

30—8 in. Salad Plate

L26—11 oz. Goblet

L26—12 oz. Ftd. Ice Tea

Plate etching decoration GOLD BROCADE
Crystal. Lotus catalog dedicated just to two lines. Circa 1950-70. Lotus was prolific and successful for decades in adding hand-applied 22 and 24 karat gold to etched patterns. With the center of this plate etching left undecorated, it has a special soft appeal when banded by gold or silver. This brochure cover appears to date to the 1950-60s. The Brocade lines used 22 karat gold for Gold Brocade and platinum for Silver Brocade. Plate, torte, $35-45; sherbet, $22-26; goblet, $26-34; cocktail, $16-20.

Plate etching decoration GEORGIAN GOLD.
Form an original Lotus catalog dedicated only to this extensive decoration, circa 1950-70. This is a style of ware Lotus was well know for in its later years.
Candy, covered, $12-18; comport, $10-14; candy, covered, 8", $14-20; sugar, $6-10; creamer, $6-10; square trays, 8" x 8", $12-20, 12" x 12", $16-24; circle trays, 8", $12-14; 12", $16-24; cocktail, 3 1/2 oz., $10-14; cordial, 1 oz., $26-36; mayo set, 3 pieces, $12-22; vase, bud, 6", $12-16, vase, bud, 10", $14-20; comport, $14-20; pitcher, 32 oz., $18-24; pitcher, 80 oz., $34-38; plate, salad, $14-20; goblet, 11 oz., $18-24; iced tea, 12 oz., $18-26; candy, covered, $20-28; juice, footed, 5 oz., $8-14; sherbet, 6 oz., $12-16; claret, 5 oz., $14-18.

**250—15 pc. Punch Set**
1 only No. 250 Bowl & Glass Ladle
12 only No. 250 Hld. Roly Poly Cup
1 only 17" Round Plate

**251/14 Snack Set**
1 only No. 251 Bowl
1 only 14" Circle

**936 Sugar & Cream with Tray**

**109/920 Martini Set**

**113/26—7 pc. Claret/Wine Set**

**928/1966 Martini Set with Tray**

**112/26—7 pc. Cordial/Brandy Set**

**111/26—3 pc. Cordial/Brandy Set**

Delicate rose filagree encrusted with 22 karat paste gold by the exclusive Lotus process. Complete assortment of hand made ringing crystal lead glass stemware, drinkware and serving pieces of finest crystal will add beauty and grace to every occasion.

Plate etching decoration ROSEATE Pattern
The cover to an illustrated promotional catalog for retail sales. Note the cover features Heisey #124 candles and #1519 Waverly pattern bowl. Circa 1950s.

Plate etching decoration GEORGIAN GOLD.
From an original Lotus catalog dedicated only to this extensive decoration, circa 1950-70. This is a style of ware Lotus was well know for in its later years. Punch set, 15 pieces, $200-240; snack set, 2 pieces, $40-60; tumbler, cut base, 14 oz., $20-24; double old fashion, $20-24; martini set, 8 pieces, $80-90; sugar and cream with tray, $26-34; candle stick, each $18-24; tray, center handled server, $22-28; martinis set, 5 pieces, $30-40; cordial/brandy set, 7 pieces, $60-80; cordial set, 3 pieces, $40-58; covered candy #931, $12-16; covered candy #929, $12-16. The Glass Blanks: Many of the pieces on this page were possibly made by Mid-Atlantic Glass such as the punch bowl and sugar, creamer, martini set components, etc. The candle stick and center handled tray are Viking's Princess line.

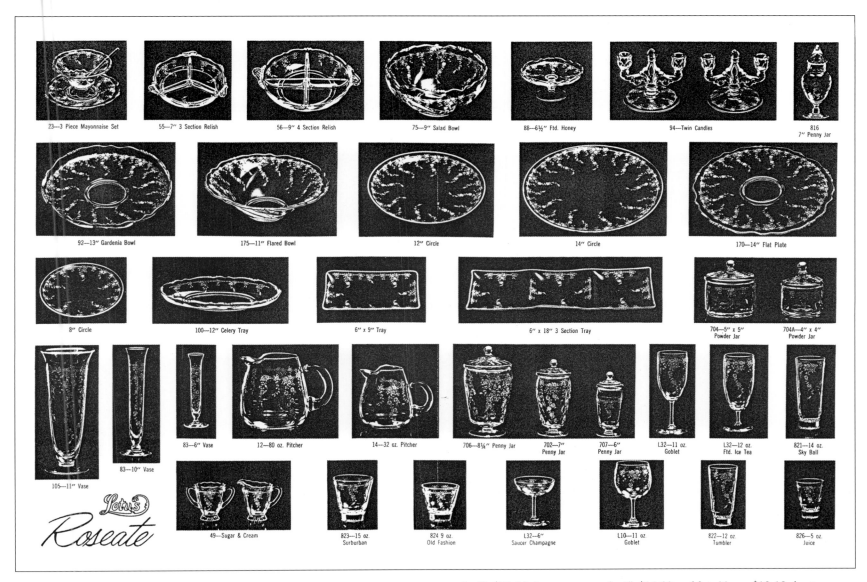

23—3 Piece Mayonnaise Set  55—7" 3 Section Relish  56—9" 4 Section Relish  75—9" Salad Bowl  88—6½" Ftd. Honey  94—Twin Candles  816 7" Penny Jar

92—13" Gardenia Bowl  175—11" Flared Bowl  12" Circle  14" Circle  170—14" Flat Plate

8" Circle  100—12" Celery Tray  6" x 9" Tray  6" x 18" 3 Section Tray  704—5" x 5" Powder Jar  704A—4" x 4" Powder Jar

83—6" Vase  12—80 oz. Pitcher  14—32 oz. Pitcher  706—8¼" Penny Jar  702—7" Penny Jar  707—6" Penny Jar  L32—11 oz. Goblet  L32—12 oz. Ftd. Ice Tea  821—14 oz. Sky Ball

83—10" Vase

105—11" Vase

Lotus Roseate

49—Sugar & Cream  823—15 oz. Surburban  824 9 oz. Old Fashion  L32—6" Saucer Champagne  L10—11 oz. Goblet  822—12 oz. Tumbler  826—5 oz. Juice

Plate etching decoration ROSEATE Pattern
Louts Glass promotional brochure, circa 1940-1957.
Mayo set, 3 piece, $24-28; relish, 3 section, $18-24; relish, 4 section, $24-28; bowl, salad, 9", $36-46; dish, footed honey, $18-24; candles stick, twin light, each $28-36; jar, penny candy with lid, $22-32; bowl, gardenia, 13", $32-38; bowl, flared, 11", $28-34; circle/tray, 12", $20-24; circle/tray, 14", $24-28; plate, flat, 14", $22-26; circle/tray, 8", $18-22; tray, celery, 12", $22-30; tray, rectangular, 6" x 9", $8-16; tray, 3 section, $14-20; jar, powder, 5", $12-16; jar, powder, 4", $10-14; vase, footed, 11", $24-32; vase, bud, 10", $12-18; vase, bud, 6", $10-16; pitcher, 80 oz., $24-36; pitcher, 32 oz., $20-28; jar, penny candy, 8 1/2", $18-26; jar, penny candy, 7", $16-24; jar, penny candy, 6", $14-20; goblet, 11 oz., $12-18; ice tea, footed, 12 oz., $12-16; tumbler, sky ball, 14 oz., $10-14; sugar, $12-16; creamer, $12-16; tumbler, suburban, 15 oz., $6-10; tumbler, old fashion, 9 oz., $6-10; saucer champagne, 6", $10-14; goblet, 11 oz., $10-18; tumbler, 12 oz., $8-12; juice, 5 oz., $4-8.
The Glass Blanks: The double candles, 11" flared bowl, gardenia bowl, footed honey, torte plate, celery tray, salad bowl, both divided relishes, and the mayo are all Heisey Waverly pattern blanks. Waverly was made by Heisey between 1940 and 1957 allowing us to date this offering to that period. The sugar and creamer are Viking Glass Princess line.

# Chapter Six

# Paint & Enamel Patterns

No. 100 - GOLDEN BLUE.

59 - 7 IN. COVERED BOWL.

59 - 6 IN. PLATE, ALSO 7 1/2 IN. SIZE.

59 - 8 IN. PLATE.

59 - 8 IN. BOWL, ALSO 9 IN. SIZES.

59. LOW FOOTED SHERBET.

59 - 6 IN. COMPORT.

59 - 1/2 LB. CANDY JAR.

59 - HIGH FOOTED SHERBET.

59 - 6 IN. BASKET.

59 - 5 IN. BASKET.

59 - 4 IN. BASKET.

59 - 9 OZ. TABLE TUMBLER.

59 - 1/2 GAL. JUG.

THE LOTUS CUT GLASS CO., BARNESVILLE, OHIO, U.S.A.

*Opposite Page:*
Decoration No. 100 GOLD BLUE Pattern
All crystal. Original Lotus catalog page pre-1924.
Bowl/candy with lid, 7", $18-28; plate, 6", $8-12 (not
shown 7 1/2", $8-14); plate, 8", $10-14; bowl, 8", $14-18
(not shown 9", $15-19); sherbet, low-footed, $6-9;
comport, 6", $8-14; candy jar with lid, 1/2 lb., $20-28;
sherbet, high-footed, $6-9; basket, 6", $35-45; basket,
5", $30-40; basket, 4", $25-35; tumbler, table, 9 oz., $8-
14; jug, 1/2 gal., $35-38.

Decoration No. 100 Golden Blue pattern. A *Keystone* magazine ad for the Gold Blue pattern, giving a production date of circa March of 1922.

Decoration No. 104
All crystal. Original Lotus catalog page, pre-1924.
Sugar or creamer, each $6-10; sugar or creamer, large, each $8-12; comport, low, $12-18; candy jar with cover, $18-28; basket, 3", $18-26; comport, high, 6", $12-19; comport, high, 7", $14-20; basket, 5", $24-34; basket, 4", $20-28; basket, 6", $36-48; basket, sugar, $24-36.

DEC. 109 LOTUS.

C8156.

1800 Hi Comp't.
Dec. 109.

1800 Covd. Comp't.
Dec. 109.

1800 Tall Comp't.
Dec. 109

1800 Mayonnaise Bowl.
Dec. 109.

420 - 8" Candle.
Dec. 106.

420 - 8" Bowl.
Dec. 106.

420 - 8" Candle.
Dec. 106.

1800 R. Edge Compott
Dec. 109.

THE LOTUS CUT GLASS COMPANY. BARNESVILLE, OHIO, USA

Decoration IRIS Pattern
All crystal. Original Lotus linen black and white photo page, circa 1940s.
Cocktail shaker with metal lid, 30 oz., $35-48; ice tub with metal handle, $30-40; bitters
bottle with metal stopper, $20-32; finger bowl/fruit, footed, $12-16; cocktail, 3 1/2 oz., $12-
16; plate, bread & butter, 6", $6-9; tumbler, footed, 9 oz., $8-10; saucer champagne, 5 1/2
oz., $10-14; plate, salad, 8", $8-10; iced tea, footed, 12 oz., $10-16.
Note: A typed note attached to this photo described this as, "Iris eight different enamel
colors, luncheon service for eight."

*Opposite Page:*
Decorations No. 109 and 106
All crystal. Original Lotus
catalog page, pre-1924.
Decoration 109 water lily
compote, high, $26-38;
compote/candy with lid, $30-
40 compote, tall, $22-32;
mayonnaise bowl, $18-26;
candle, 8", each $18-28; bowl,
console, decoration 106, $18-
28; comport, rolled edge,
decoration 109, $20-32.

Decoration POPPY Design
All ebony/"black glass" original Lotus Cut Glass Co. catalog page, pre-1924.
Candy/chocolate box with lid, 6", $40-54; flower block/frog, 4", $20-30 (not shown 5",
$22-34); card tray, three-toed, 7", $20-26; cigarette box with ash tray lid, 5 3/4", $50-58;
bowl, bulb, 6", $20-28; comport, low-footed, 8 1/2", $30-38; cheese & cracker, two part,
10", $30-44; comport, high-footed, 7 1/2", $34-42.

The Lotus Cut Glass Co. Barnesville, Ohio.

No. 307 Vase Azurite
Dec. 114.

309 Vase Primrose
Dec. 114.

304. Vase Primrose
Dec. 114.

305 Vase Ivory
Dec. 114.

306 . Vase . Dec 114 .

303 . Vase Helio.
Dec. 114.

308 Vase Helio
Dec. 114.

301 Vase Ebony
Dec. 114.

302. Vase Azurite
Dec. 114.

Decoration AUTUMN Pattern
Crystal gold and hand painted pink.
Undated magazine page advertisement - no prices established.
Note: This is one of many 1950s-60s color decorations in this style. It is only
an example of several extensive lines from this era.

Decoration #114.
Gold band on opaque glass,
original Lotus Cut Glass
catalog page, pre-1924.
Vase, ivory, #303, $62-68;
vase, crimped, #307, $58-
62; vase, primrose, #309,
$58-62; vase, primrose,
#304, $62-68; vase,
primrose, #306, $52-58;
vase, helio, #303, $62-68;
vase, helio, #308, $65-75;
vase, ebony, #301, $60-72;
vase, azurite, #302, $68-72.
The Glass Blanks: The
forms and color names are
all Cambridge Glass.

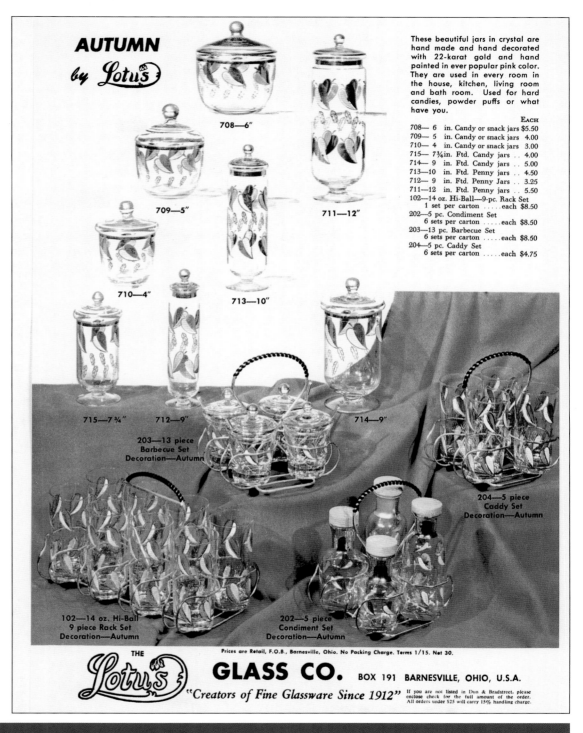

AUTUMN by Lotus

These beautiful jars in crystal are hand made and hand decorated with 22-karat gold and hand painted in ever popular pink color. They are used in every room in the house, kitchen, living room and bath room. Used for hard candies, powder puffs or what have you.

EACH
708— 6 in. Candy or snack jars $5.50
709— 5 in. Candy or snack jars 4.00
710— 4 in. Candy or snack jars 3.00
715— 7¾ in. Ftd. Candy jars .. 4.00
714— 9 in. Ftd. Candy jars .. 5.00
713—10 in. Ftd. Penny jars 4.50
712— 9 in. Ftd. Penny Jars 3.25
711—12 in. Ftd. Penny jars .. 5.50
102—14 oz. Hi-Ball—9-pc. Rack Set
    1 set per carton .....each $8.50
202—5 pc. Condiment Set
    6 sets per carton .....each $8.50
203—13 pc. Barbecue Set
    6 sets per carton .....each $8.50
204—5 pc. Caddy Set
    6 sets per carton .....each $4.75

708—6"
709—5"
711—12"
710—4"
713—10"
715—7¾"
712—9"
714—9"
203—13 piece Barbecue Set Decoration—Autumn
204—5 piece Caddy Set Decoration—Autumn
102—14 oz. Hi-Ball 9 piece Rack Set Decoration—Autumn
202—5 piece Condiment Set Decoration—Autumn

Prices are Retail, F.O.B., Barnesville, Ohio. No Packing Charge. Terms 1/15. Net 30.

THE Lotus GLASS CO. BOX 191 BARNESVILLE, OHIO, U.S.A.
"Creators of Fine Glassware Since 1912"
If you are not listed in Dun & Bradstreet, please enclose check for the full amount of the order. All orders under $25 will carry 15% handling charge.

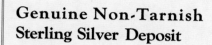

## Genuine Non-Tarnish Sterling Silver Deposit

*Sylvania Decoration No. 54*

### DECORATIVE GLASSWARE
Ebony and Crystal

### THE LOTUS GLASS CO., Inc.
Barnesville, Ohio

*DECORATORS OF HIGH GRADE*
*GLASSWARE SINCE 1912*

**LOTUS GENUINE NON-TARNISH STERLING SILVER DEPOSIT**
retains forever its original beauty and polish

Smartly designed in useful and decorative
pieces for every purpose

| | | | Retail Price Each |
|---|---|---|---|
| 7654 | 11½ in. | Flat Rim Vase | $ 7.00 |
| 6554 | 4¾ in. | 2-Light Candle | 12.00 |
| 7154 | 7 in. | Tall Comport | 5.50 |
| 7254 | 8¾ in. | Rose Bowl | 7.00 |
| 9754 | 10 in. | Cheese and Cracker | 5.50 |
| 9554 | 3½ in. | Low Candle (pair) | 5.50 |
| 7454 | 12 in. | 6-Toe Flared Bowl | 6.50 |
| 8854 | 9 in. | 2-Handled Bell Bowl | 5.50 |
| 8954 | 11 in. | 2-Handled Sandwich | 5.50 |
| 9854 | 10 in. | Handled Cake Tray | 5.50 |

### THE LOTUS GLASS CO., Inc.
Barnesville, Ohio

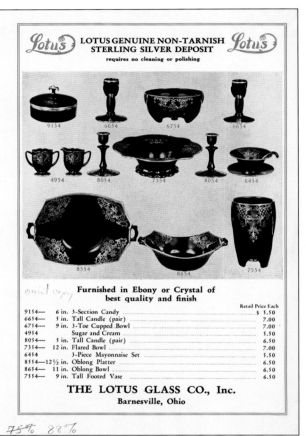

**LOTUS GENUINE NON-TARNISH STERLING SILVER DEPOSIT**
requires no cleaning or polishing

Furnished in Ebony or Crystal of
best quality and finish

| | | | Retail Price Each |
|---|---|---|---|
| 9154 | 6 in. | 3-Section Candy | $ 5.50 |
| 6654 | 5 in. | Tall Candle (pair) | 7.00 |
| 6754 | 9 in. | 3-Toe Cupped Bowl | 7.00 |
| 4954 | | Sugar and Cream | 5.50 |
| 8054 | 5 in. | Tall Candle (pair) | 6.50 |
| 7354 | 12 in. | Flared Bowl | 7.00 |
| 6454 | | 3-Piece Mayonnaise Set | 5.50 |
| 8554 | 12½ in. | Oblong Platter | 6.50 |
| 8654 | 11 in. | Oblong Bowl | 6.50 |
| 7554 | 9 in. | Tall Footed Vase | 6.50 |

### THE LOTUS GLASS CO., Inc.
Barnesville, Ohio

Decoration No. 54 SYLVANIA Pattern

Black Glass with Sterling Silver, also offered crystal. Crystal valued approximately 30% of black. Lotus retail flier, circa 1930s.

Vase, flat rim, 11 1/2", $100-125; candlestick, two light, 4 3/4", $50-75; comport, tall, 7", $30-48; rose bowl, 8 3/4", $65-85; cheese and cracker, two part, 10", $40-65; candle, low, 3 1/2", each $24-36; bowl, flared, six-toed, $60-75; bowl, two open handled, bell, $36-48; plate, sandwich, two open handled, 11", $34-46; plate, cake, center handled server, 10", $40-58; (Second image) candy, 3 part with lid, 6", $50-68; candle, tall, 5", each $50-75; bowl, cupped, three-toed, 9", $70-85; cream and sugar, each $22-32; candle, tall, 5", each $35-48; bowl, flared, 12", $65-78; mayonnaise set, 3 piece, $50-65; platter, oblong, two open handles, 12 1/2", $40-58; bowl, oblong, 11", $60-85; vase, tall-footed/3-toed, 9", $80-95.

The Glass Blanks: This offering seems to be a healthy mix of Duncan and Miller and Central Glass. The low candle stick and six-toed console bowl, probably the cheese and cracker as well as the open handled bowl and plate on the first page, are Central. The covered candy, mayo set, and two open handled pieces on the bottom row are Central as well. All other forms can be attributed to Duncan & Miller Glass.

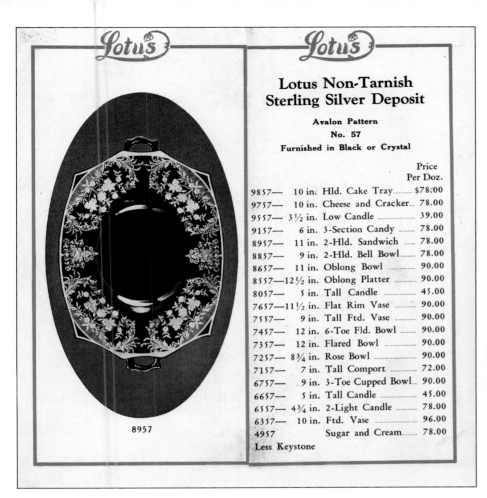

Lotus

Lotus

## Lotus Non-Tarnish Sterling Silver Deposit

**Avalon Pattern**
**No. 57**
**Furnished in Black or Crystal**

| | | | Price Per Doz. |
|---|---|---|---|
| 9857— | 10 in. | Hld. Cake Tray | $78.00 |
| 9757— | 10 in. | Cheese and Cracker | 78.00 |
| 9557— | 3½ in. | Low Candle | 39.00 |
| 9157— | 6 in. | 3-Section Candy | 78.00 |
| 8957— | 11 in. | 2-Hld. Sandwich | 78.00 |
| 8857— | 9 in. | 2-Hld. Bell Bowl | 78.00 |
| 8657— | 11 in. | Oblong Bowl | 90.00 |
| 8557— | 12½ in. | Oblong Platter | 90.00 |
| 8057— | 5 in. | Tall Candle | 45.00 |
| 7657— | 11½ in. | Flat Rim Vase | 90.00 |
| 7557— | 9 in. | Tall Ftd. Vase | 90.00 |
| 7457— | 12 in. | 6-Toe Fld. Bowl | 90.00 |
| 7357— | 12 in. | Flared Bowl | 90.00 |
| 7257— | 8¾ in. | Rose Bowl | 90.00 |
| 7157— | 7 in. | Tall Comport | 72.00 |
| 6757— | 9 in. | 3-Toe Cupped Bowl | 90.00 |
| 6657— | 5 in. | Tall Candle | 45.00 |
| 6557— | 4¾ in. | 2-Light Candle | 78.00 |
| 6357— | 10 in. | Ftd. Vase | 96.00 |
| 4957— | | Sugar and Cream | 78.00 |

**Less Keystone**

8957

Decoration No. 57 AVALON Pattern
Black Glass with Sterling Silver. Crystal also produced
and would be roughly 30% of the value of black.
Original Lotus point of purchase brochure. Only the
oblong platter is illustrated, $60-85.

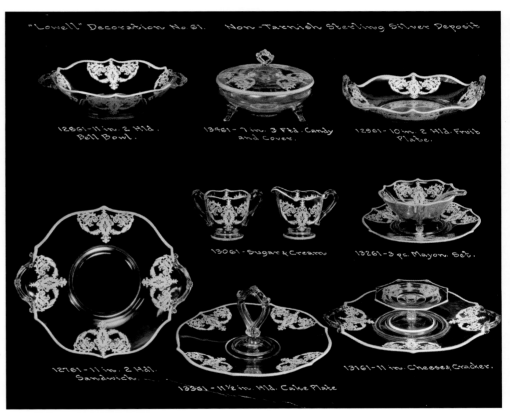

Decoration No. 61 LOWELL Pattern
Crystal with Sterling Silver.
Bowl, bell, two handled, 11", $18-24; candy, three-footed with lid, 7", $20-28; plate, fruit, two handled, 10", $16-22; sugar or creamer, each $10-16; mayonnaise set, three piece, $20-32; plate, sandwich, two handled, 11", $18-24; plate, cake, center handled server, 11 1/2", $18-26; cheese and cracker, two part, 11", $20-38.
The Glass Blanks: All pieces shown here appear to be Lancaster Glass blanks.

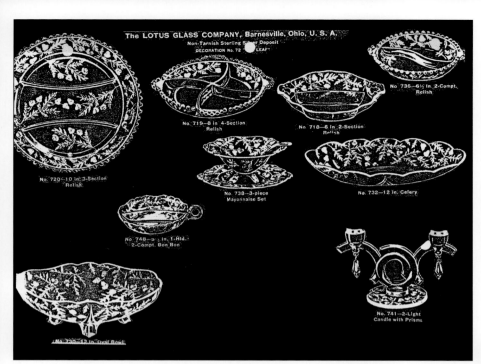

Decoration No. 72 OAK LEAF Pattern
Crystal with Sterling Silver.
3 part relish, 10", $45-54; 4 section relish, 8", $36-42; 2 part relish, 6", $20-26; 2 part relish, 6 1/2", $20-24; mayo set, 3 part, $24-29; celery, 12", $28-32; bonbon, 2 compartment, handled, $20-24; bowl, oval, 12", $42-48; candle with prisms, 2 light, $78-86.
Note: This page is one of three in the text created from largely illegible originals. The use of compromised images is regretted; but, the importance of the pattern and use of these blanks, illustrated in the material available to me nowhere else, was deemed important enough to make this cut and paste composite page, made from three originals, worthwhile.
The Glass Blanks: The three beaded edge relishes on the top row are all Imperial Glass Candlewick line blanks. All other pieces are Cambridge glass.

Decoration No. 72 OAK LEAF Pattern
Crystal with Sterling Silver.
2-light candle with prisms, $110-120; twin/two part mayo, $30-34; plate, handled, 7", $18-26; triple candle, each $74-84; relish, two tab handles, $28-34; 2 light candle, each $60-68; two tab handled bowl, $66-74; cheese plate, 1 handle, 6", $14-18.
Note: This page is one of three in the text created from largely illegible originals. The use of compromised images is regretted; but, the importance of the pattern and use of these blanks, illustrated in the material available to me nowhere else, was deemed important enough to make this cut and paste composite page, made from three originals, worthwhile.
The Glass Blanks: All of the pieces selected for this created page are Heisey Glass.

Decoration No. 73 VINTAGE Pattern
Crystal with Sterling Silver.
Lotus original catalog page.
Candle, two light, 6", each $24-38; bowl, orange, three-toed, 11", $20-38; sugar
or cream, each $12-18; celery tray, 11", $14-22; candle, three light, 6", $28-42;
bowl, centerpiece, 10 1/2", $20-38; bonbon, footed with lid, 6", $24-38; comport,
6 1/2", $20-32; cheese and cracker, two part, 10", $22-38; plate, cake, center
handled server/tray, 12", $24-38; mayo, 3 piece, $24-28; candle, 3", each $12-16;
rose bowl, three-toed, 6 1/2", $28-38; vase, footed, crimped, 9 1/2", $32-44.
The Glass Blanks: All of these pieces are Tiffin Glass line 3248.

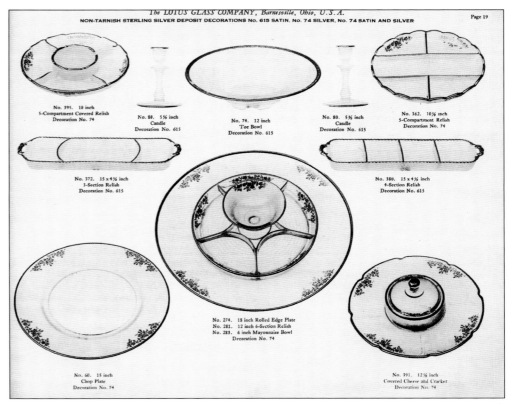

Decoration No. 74 and 615
Crystal with Sterling Silver.
The suggested values are for the pieces as shown. For pieces with silver deposit
and satin add 20-40% over the silver-edged only pieces.
Relish, 5 part, deco. 74, $25-38; candlesticks, deco. 615, each $12-20; toe bowl,
decoration 615, $10-22; relish, 5 part, deco. 74, $24-36; 3 section relish, deco.
615, $15-22; relish, 4 section, deco. 615, $15-22; chop plate, deco. 74, $15-28;
rolled edge plate, deco. 74, $25-38; relish, 6 section, deco. 74, $25-38; mayonnaise bowl, deco. 74, $12-20; cheese and cracker with lid, deco. 74, $30-34.
Note: The satin and silver pieces are most desirable. While 615 appears as satin
finish with a sterling edge decoration and 74 as shown is silver deposit flowers
and satin, it might be assumed that No. 74 silver is the silver edge treatments
without satin. None of the satin only pieces appear on this page.

No. 295. 6 inch
Handled 3-Section Relish
Decoration No. 74

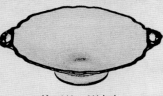

No. 366. 6½ inch
2-Handled Comport
Decoration No. 615

No. 376. 11 inch
2-Section Relish
Decoration No. 615

No. 367. 6 inch
2-Handled Comport
Decoration No. 615

No. 371
Honey Box and Lid
Decoration No. 615

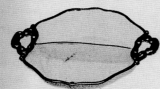

No. 324. 8½ inch
Relish
Decoration No. 615

No. 374. 7 inch
2-Handled
2-Section Relish
Decoration No. 615

No. 323. 8 inch Relish
Decoration No. 74

No. 368. 6½ inch
Handled 3-Compartment Relish
Decoration No. 615

No. 379. 4½ inch
Sugar Basket
Decoration No. 615

No. 325
3-Light Candle
Decoration No. 615

No. 394. Oval Bowl
Decoration No. 615

No. 325
3-Light Candle
Decoration No. 615

No. 399. 8 inch
2-Section Relish
Decoration No. 615

No. 375. 9 inch
2-Section Relish
Decoration No. 615

No. 293. 6 inch
3-Section Relish
Decoration No. 74

No. 361. 6 inch
Center Handled Relish
Decoration No. 615

No. 365
4-Piece Mayonnaise Set
Decoration No. 74

No. 370. 8 inch
4-Compartment Relish
Decoration No. 615

*Opposite Page:*

Decoration No. 74 and 615 continued.

Crystal with Sterling Silver. The suggested values are for the pieces as shown. For pieces with silver deposit and satin add 20-40% over the silver-edged only pieces. The large oval bowl, $36-48; the three light candle sticks, each $30-38; there are four small serving pieces shown in decoration No. 74, each $12-24; all other pieces in crystal and satin only, $8-14 each.

The Glass Blanks: Many of the pieces on this page are Cambridge Glass lines 3500 and 3400. All of the first row, excluding the 3 part relish, is Cambridge. On the second row, items 374, 368, and 379, and further down, items 375, 361, and 370 are Cambridge. The 4 part mayo on the bottom is Cambridge line #1402 Tally Ho. Exceptions are the winged large oval bowl and candle sticks which are Duncan's 314 and the relish numbered here 323 is New Martinsville Glass 337 Moondrops line.

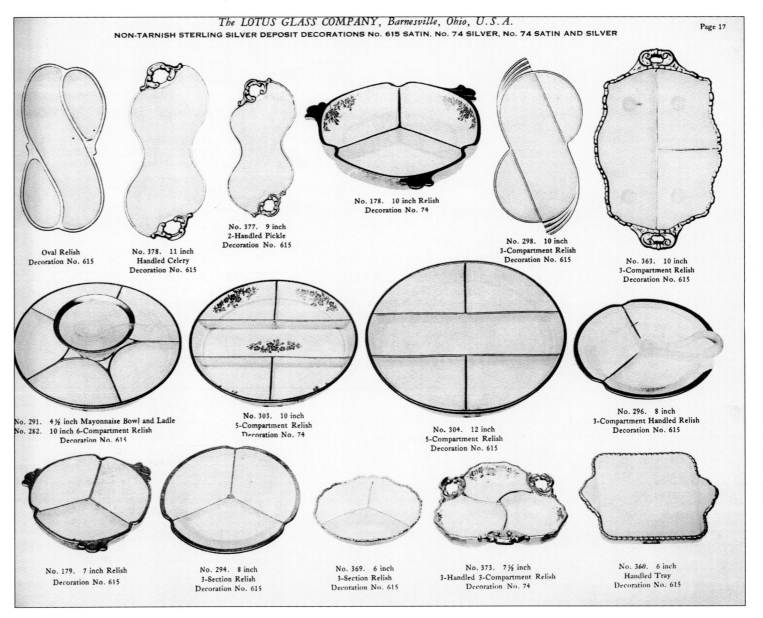

The LOTUS GLASS COMPANY, Barnesville, Ohio, U.S.A.

NON-TARNISH STERLING SILVER DEPOSIT DECORATIONS No. 615 SATIN. No. 74 SILVER, No. 74 SATIN AND SILVER

Page 17

Oval Relish
Decoration No. 615

No. 378. 11 inch
Handled Celery
Decoration No. 615

No. 377. 9 inch
2-Handled Pickle
Decoration No. 615

No. 178. 10 inch Relish
Decoration No. 74

No. 298. 10 inch
3-Compartment Relish
Decoration No. 615

No. 363. 10 inch
3-Compartment Relish
Decoration No. 615

No. 291. 4½ inch Mayonnaise Bowl and Ladle
No. 282. 10 inch 6-Compartment Relish
Decoration No. 615

No. 303. 10 inch
5-Compartment Relish
Decoration No. 74

No. 304. 12 inch
5-Compartment Relish
Decoration No. 615

No. 296. 8 inch
3-Compartment Handled Relish
Decoration No. 615

No. 179. 7 inch Relish
Decoration No. 615

No. 294. 8 inch
3-Section Relish
Decoration No. 615

No. 369. 6 inch
3-Section Relish
Decoration No. 615

No. 373. 7½ inch
3-Handled 3-Compartment Relish
Decoration No. 74

No. 360. 6 inch
Handled Tray
Decoration No. 615

Decoration No. 74 and 615 continued.
Crystal with Sterling Silver.
The suggested values are for the pieces as shown. For pieces with silver deposit and satin add 20-40% over the silver-edged only pieces.
Three divided relish trays are show here with decoration No. 74, each $18-32; all other satin and silver only pieces, each $14-26.

No. 610—7 in.
Comport

No. 604—7 in.
Shell Comport

No. 481—4 in.
Salt and Pepper

No. 482—5 in.
Salt and Pepper

No. 616—9 in.
Oval Tray

No. 614—8 in.
2-Hld. Plate

No. 615—6 in.
Square 2-Hld. Plate

No. 608—8½ in.
3-Toed Plate

No. 605—4½ in.
Shell 3-Toed Bon Bon

No. 609—8½ in.
3-Toed Deep Bon Bon

No. 606—7 in.
3-Toed Bon Bon

No. 469
Twin Mayonnaise Set

No. 611—8½ in.
3-Compt. Relish

No. 607—9 in.
3-Compt. Relish

No. 612—6 in.
2-Compt. Relish

No. 613
3-pc. Salad Set

Decoration No. 75 IVY Pattern.
Crystal with Sterling Silver.
Lotus original catalog page.
Comport, 7", $16-28; comport, shell, 7", $18-28; salt and pepper, pair, 4", $14-18; salt and pepper, pair, 5", $16-22; plate, square, two handled, 6", $12-18; plate, footed, two handled, 8", $20-32; plate, three-toed, 8 1/2", $18-28; tray, oval, 9", $18-26; bonbon, shell, three-toed, 4 1/2", $16-24; bonbon, three-toed, deep, 8 1/2", $14-28; bonbon, three-toed, 7", $16-28; mayonnaise set, two pieces, $28-38; relish, three part, 8 1/2", $20-32; relish, 3 compartment shell, three-toed, 9", $22-38; relish, two compartment, 6", $16-26; bowl/salad set, 3 pieces, $20-28.
The Glass Blanks: Most of this page is Cambridge Glass. The shakers are by an unidentified manufacturer and the twin mayo is Heisey line #3397 Gascony. All else is Cambridge. The pieces with shell forms are from the Cambridge Seashell line, also called Krystol Shell at times. The other pieces are from the Cambridge Caprice line.

Decoration No. 75 IVY Pattern.
Crystal with Sterling Silver.
Lotus original catalog page.
Candle, 5", each $12-20; candle, two light, each $22-38; candle and prisms, 5", $30-50; candle, three light (note captions and images inverted in original catalog), each $35-58; sugar and creamer, each $8-14; French Dressing bottle with stopper, $18-28; oil bottle/cruet with original stopper, $20-32; syrup with metal lid, $14-28; cereal jug, $30-46; marmalade jar with lid, $18-29; sugar, cream, and tray, 3 piece set, $32-50; lemon, oval with lid, 6 1/2", $20-32; plate, chop, four-toed, $22-36; bowl, footed, flared, 11", $30-48; bowl, footed, flared, 9", $28-32; bowl, shell, three-toed, 10", $34-48; comport, footed, shell, 9", $32-46.
The Glass Blanks: All of the candlesticks are Cambridge Glass. The sugar and cream are Heisey New Era line #4044. The dressing bottle, oil bottle, and syrup are Heisey. The cereal jug is Heisey Twentieth Century line, the Marmalade is Heisey #1183 Revere line, and the sugar and creamer on tray and oval lemon are Heisey Empress #1401 line. The bottom of the page contains all Cambridge Caprice and Seashell lines.

No. 621—5 in.
Candle

No. 619—6 in.
2-Light Candle

No. 620—5 in.
Candle and Prism

No. 618—5 in.
3-Light Candle

No. 471
Sugar and Cream

No. 476
French Dressing Bottle

No. 475
Oil Bottle

No. 477
Syrup

No. 479
Cereal Jug

No. 474
Marmalade and Cover

No. 470
Sugar, Cream and Tray

No. 472—6½ in.
Oval Lemon and Cover

No. 600—11 in.
Footed Flared Bowl

No. 601—9 in.
Flared Bowl

No. 617—14 in.
Chop Plate

No. 602—10 in. Shell
3-Toed Bowl

No. 603—9 in.
Shell Comport

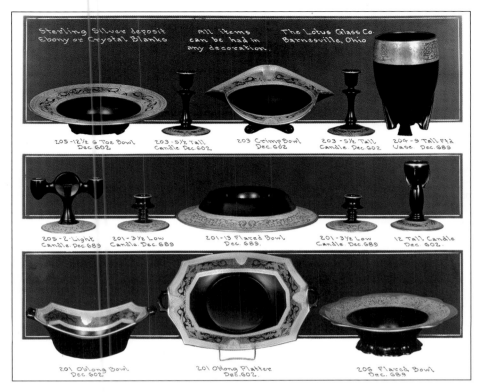

Decoration No. 602 and 689
Ebony/black glass with Sterling Silver. Also noted as made in Crystal, which would be approximately 25-30% of the value of black, as suggested.
Lotus original catalog page. Circa 1930s. Prices for shape do not vary with changes from decoration 689 to 602.
Bowl, 6-toed, 12 1/2", $58-70; candle, tall, 5 1/2", each $35-42; bowl, three-crimped, three-toed, $50-65; vase, tall, three-footed, $80-95; candle, two light, each $40-50; candle, low, 3 1/2", $25-30; bowl, flared console, 13", $55-70; candle, tall, each $38-48; bowl, oblong, two open handles, $60-68; platter, oblong, two open handles, $60-68; bowl, flared, $60-68.
The Glass Blanks: The low stick on the second row is Central #2000, the flared rim console bowl is Central #2000 bowl, and the oblong plate and platter on the bottom row are Central #2002. Duncan pieces include the three toe bowl from the Three Leaf line, the three-footed tall vase is their #12, the 12" tall candle was introduced in 1930 by Duncan, and the 2 light is Duncan #21 Plaza.

Decoration No. 602, 689, and 695
Ebony/black glass with Sterling Silver. Also noted as made in Crystal, which would be approximately 25-30% of the value of black as suggested.
Lotus original catalog page. Prices for shape do not vary with changes from decoration 689 or 695; however, 690 might be more desirable. Priced as shown.
Rose bowl, $58-65; bowl, flower, flat rim, three-toed, $65-85; vase, large-footed, $65-80; whip cream/mayonnaise, 3 pieces set, $45-65; candle, tall, 5 1/2", each $40-45; bowl, fruit, footed, $60-75; relish/candy with lid, 6", $40-58; plate, cake, center handled serving tray, 10", $45-58; cheese and cracker, two part, 10", $45-60; pan/bowl, lily, $40-55.
The Glass Blanks: The flat rim flower bowl is Duncan & Miller. The tall candlesticks, the footed fruit bowl, and the covered relish/candy box are all Central glass products. The rose bowl is Duncan's #8 bowl.

Decorated CALL OF THE WILD Pattern
Ebony/black glass with Sterling Silver. Original Lotus catalog page, pattern introduced 1930.
Mayonnaise, three piece, $160-180; candle, tall, #8050, each $80-100; candle, low, each $60-75; candle, tall, #6650, each $100-120; candy box with lid, open finial, $150-160; candle, double, each $140-160; bowl, three-toed, cupped, $180-200; vase, three-toed, cupped, $210-240; bowl, flower, flat-rimmed, three-toed, $200-230; comport, tall, $85-95.
Note: An illustrated advertisement appears in *The Pottery, Glass & Brass Salesman* of October 1930 showing Call of the Wild and calls it, "the very newest and of the most profitable achievements by Lotus." It is noted as available on black or crystal glass.
The Glass Blanks: the 6650 candlestick is Duncan, as are the 3 three-toed pieces, and the 6550 two light candle, which is #21 Plaza line. The #5050 covered candy is Duncan's item #106, 3 compartment candy, shown in Weatherman as a 1943 catalog reprint. Possibly other pieces on this page are Duncan as well.

Decorated CALL OF THE WILD Pattern
Ebony/black glass with Sterling Silver. Original Lotus catalog page, pattern introduced 1930.
Bowl, flared, 12", $140-160; rose bowl, 8 3/4", $160-180; bowl, flared, six-toed, 12 1/2", $150-170; vase, 8", $120-140; candlestick, winged, 5 1/2", each $120-140; bowl, winged, $220-250; vase, 6", $120-130; candy box, round with lid, 6", $135-150; plate, cake, center handled serving tray, 10", $120-145; cheese and cracker, two part, 10", $120-135.
The Glass Blanks: The wing candlestick 6850 is Duncan No. 16, as is the winged bowl. The first two bowls at the top right are Duncan's #8. The covered candy is Central Glass #2005. Probably other pieces are Central and Duncan as well.

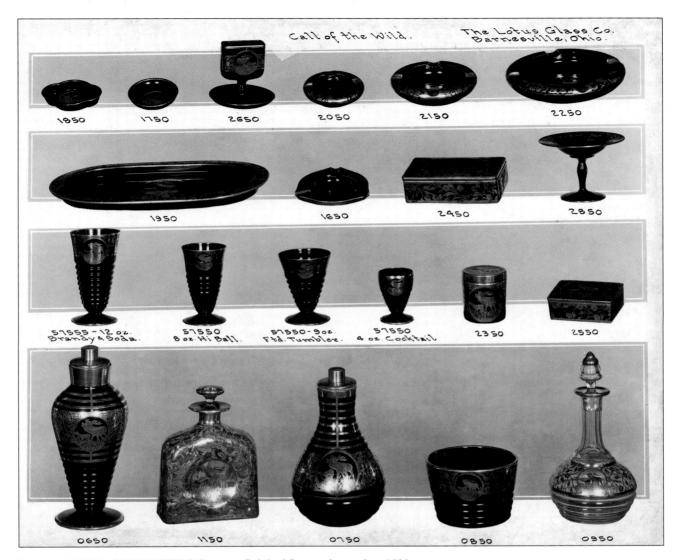

Decorated CALL OF THE WILD Pattern. Original Lotus photo, circa 1930s.
Ebony/black glass with Sterling Silver, two pieces of decorated crystal. Original Lotus catalog page, pattern introduced 1930.
Pin tray, lobed, $40-58; pin tray, round, $30-40; card/cigarette holder, $180-195; ash tray, small, $40-48; ash tray, medium, $45-55; ash tray, large, $55-65: tray, oblong, $80-95; ash tray, triangular, $40-48; cigarette box with lid, $130-155; comport, small, $85-95; tumbler, brandy & soda, 12 oz., $60-68; tumbler, footed, hi ball, 8 oz., $48-58; tumbler, footed, 9 oz., $48-58; tumbler, footed, 4 oz. cocktail, $45-55; cigarette box, round with lid, $160-175; cigarette box, small with lid, $120-135; cocktail shaker, footed with metal lid, #0650, $185-210; decanter with stopper (crystal), $230-260; cocktail shaker with metal lid, #0750, $230-265; ice tub, $155-170; decanter with stopper (crystal), $140-165.
The Glass Blanks: The decanter with crystal stopper on the bottom right is Bryce Glass. The pin tray is called an ash tray in a Duncan & Miller catalog, listed as item #18. The #1650 ash tray is Duncan item #16.

1450

2427

12095·k

1211

1849

4105

EBONY SILVER LOLA

2297/12

Decorated LOLA Pattern
Ebony/black glass with Sterling Silver.
Original Lotus photo, circa 1930s.
Cream and sugar, each $24-30;
cigarette box, double with lid, $60-75;
plate, cake, center handled serving
tray, $40-50; ice bucket with metal
handle, $68-76; vase #4105, $64-72;
bowl, flared, $55-65.
The Glass Blanks: The cream and
sugar are Central Glass line #1450 and
the toed bowl appears not to be
Central's six-toed item, but, possibly,
Fostoria's three-toed console bowl?

Decorated LOLA Pattern
continued
Ebony/black glass with
Sterling Silver. Original
Lotus photo, circa 1930s.
Cheese and cracker, two part,
$50-60; candy box with lid,
round, $55-65; vase, three-
toed, $70-80; candle stick,
low, each $24-28; bowl,
console, flared, $55-65.
The Glass Blanks; The three-
toed vase is Duncan.

12097·k

1800

1900

2324/4

12

EBONY
SILVER LOLA

1900

Decorated LOLA Pattern
Crystal with Sterling Silver. Original Lotus catalog page, 1930s.
Cheese and cracker, two part, $30-36; mayonnaise/whipped cream, two
part, $30-38; plate, cake, center handled server tray, $28-36; bowl, ribbed,
$32-40; bowl, flower with frog, $75-80; salad set, two part, $45-50.

Decorated LOLA Pattern continued
Crystal with Sterling Silver. Original Lotus catalog page, circa 1930s.
Candle, low, each $22-28; comport, low, $28-34; bowl, flared rim, $46-54; tray, oblong, two
open handled, $40-46; bowl, flared rim, $38-44, bowl, two open handles, $40-46.
The Glass Blanks: The two open handled pieces appear to be Central Glass line #2002.

981

1013

835

1002

1001A

1000

SILVER LOLA

1004

Decorated LOLA Pattern
Crystal with Sterling Silver. Original Lotus catalog page, circa 1930s.
Relish, oblong, divided three part, $32-38; candy box, round with cover, $30-36; sugar
with lid, $20-25; cream, $18-22; candle stick, low, three-toed, each $22-26; vase,
footed, $50-56; ice bucket with metal handle, $34-40; bowl, flared, three-toed, $50-56.
The Glass Blanks: The footed vase 101A is Fostoria Glass Co.'s 32369, the handled ice
bucket appears to Fostoria #2378, and the three-toed bowl 1004 is Fostoria's #2394.
The cream and sugar are Heisey Revere line.

# Chapter Eight
# Decorated Tumblers

The following pages illustrated a significant part of the post 1950 Lotus production. Certainly elegant high end glassware continued to be decorated at Lotus as well as the decorated tumblers that were a huge market for many glass firms. Current pricing for individual tumblers is not provided here. There simply is not enough data on sales to support individual pricing trends. Generally these can be found on the market for $1-5 each. Some patterns and lines, such as Willow (to coordinate with Blue Willow dinnerware) or Black Gold (used on the set of TV's "Dallas"), have a significant following as distinctive patterns and may demand higher prices in select markets. At present, collecting mid-century tumblers remains an inexpensive and fun collecting field. These page in no way represent the total pattern catalog from Lotus—many, many others were created. These are included here because little has been put in print to date and young and new collectors are finding them, intrigued by their period turquoise or pink or whatever designs, and want to learn more. This chapter is only is a teaser and introduction for a topic that someone else shall need to address in the years ahead.

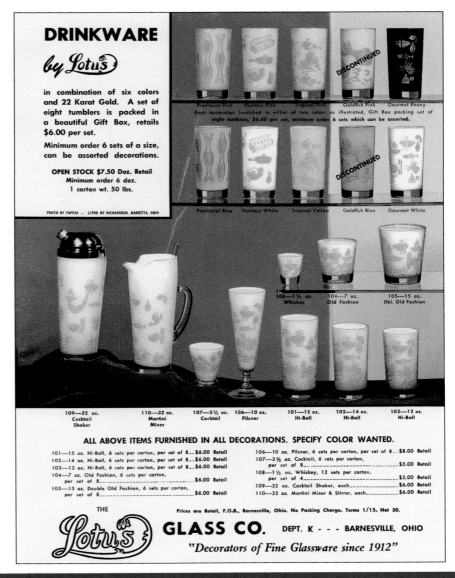

## PRESENTS

### bon apetite

This is a redesigning of the Gourmet decoration, no inside color. The panel which allows the contents of the glass to be seen is available in either Black or White and the improved design is brilliant gold.

| | | | | |
|---|---|---|---|---|
| 102—14 oz. | Hi-Ball | Set of 8 | $4.50 | 6 sets |
| 821—14 oz. | Sky Ball | Set of 8 | 5.50 | 6 sets |
| 822—12 oz. | Hi-Ball | Set of 8 | 4.50 | 6 sets |
| 823—13 oz. | Suburban | Set of 8 | 5.50 | 6 sets |
| 824—9 oz. | On the Rocks | Set of 8 | 4.50 | 6 sets |
| 825—4 oz. | Cocktail | Set of 8 | 4.50 | 6 sets |

All items shown will be packed in sets of 8 to an air cell carton. 6 sets to a master carton.

UPPER PICTURE

**Martini Set**—8 piece $6.50. Includes 1—32 oz. Martini Mixer and Stirrer and 6-525 —4 oz. Martini Cocktails Packed in Air Cell Cartons.

LOWER PICTURE

**102**—9 pc. Caddy Set $6.00. Composed of 1 Center Handled Rack and 8— 102—14 oz. Hi-Balls.

| Sky Ball 821—14 oz. | Hi-Ball 102—14 oz. | Hi-Ball 822—12 oz. | Suburban 823—13 oz. | On The Rocks 824—9 oz. | Cocktail 825—4 oz. |

Prices are Retail, F.O.B. Barnesville, Ohio. No Packing Charge. Terms 1/15. Net 30.

## GLASS CO. BOX 191 BARNESVILLE, OHIO, U.S.A.

---

### bon apetite  *now correlated by Lotus*

This fast selling Bon Apetite design by Lotus has proven so popular that the company now makes it available in bentware, drinkware, candy, snack and penny jars. This brilliant 22 karat gold design, complemented by the snow white background on Florentine Crystal will add beauty and decor to any occasion. For the hostess who is looking for service as well as beauty remember this, another Lotus product, made by a company with 46 years of fine glassware experience. Guaranteed against detergents or scrubbing.

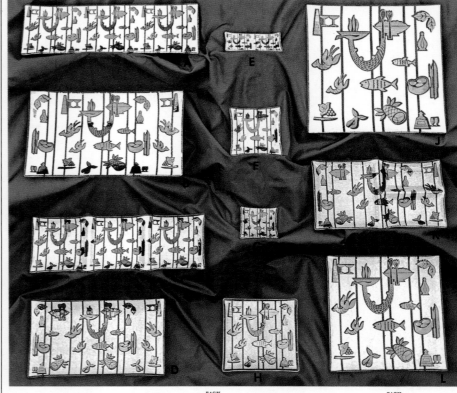

| | | EACH | | | EACH |
|---|---|---|---|---|---|
| A— | 6 x 18" Rectangle Hors d'oevure | $5.75 | G— | 4" Square Coaster or Ash Tray | $1.00 |
| B— | 10 x 16" Rectangle Sandwich Tray | 5.75 | H— | 8" Square Cake Plate | 2.75 |
| C— | 6 x 18" 3 Section Relish | 5.75 | J— | 14" Square Cake Plate | 7.50 |
| D— | 8 x 14" Rectangle Canape Tray | 4.75 | K— | 8 x 14" 3-Section Relish | 4.75 |
| E— | 3 x 6" Oblong Ash Tray or Mint | 1.00 | L— | 12" Square Cake Plate | 6.50 |
| F—5½" | Square Mint or Canape | 1.50 | | | |

Prices are Retail, F.O.B. Barnesville, Ohio. No Packing Charge. Terms 1/15. Net 30.

 **GLASS CO.** BOX 191 BARNESVILLE, OHIO, U.S.A.

If you are not listed in Dun & Bradstreet, please

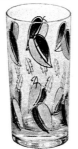

# Crystal Gems by Lotus

WILLOW

FOLKLORE

EVENING ROSE

VILLAGE

ROSE CHINTZ

WREATH

CANDLE

STRAWBERRY

BLUEBERRY

PETTIFLORA

BOWKNOT

THE Lotus Glass Co. — BARNESVILLE, OHIO 43713

# Crystal Gems by Lotus

MUSHROOM YELLOW

MUSHROOM PINK

MUSHROOM AVOCADO

MUSHROOM ORANGE

POPPY BLUE W/GREEN

POPPY RED W/GREEN

POPPY BLUE W/GOLD

POPPY YELLOW W/GOLD

POPPY YELLOW W/GREEN

POPPY GREEN W/GOLD

POPPY GREEN W/GREEN

POPPY RED W/GOLD

NAVAJO

CHEROKEE

APACHE

ZUNI

BLACKFOOT

COCKEREL

BUTTERFLY

SHASTA

BROWN EYES

PARADISE RED

PARADISE GREEN

GOLD OAK
SILVER OAK
WHITE OAK

THE Lotus Glass Co. — BARNESVILLE, OHIO 43713

# Crystal Gems *by* Lotus

| MUSHROOM YELLOW | ROSEBUD PINK | MUSHROOM AVOCADO | ROSEBUD RED | HOLLY | POINSETTIA | MERRY CHRISTMAS/ HAPPY NEW YEAR |

| ROSEBUD YELLOW | ROSEBUD WHITE | TIGER | COCKEREL | MANDARIN | ROSENE |

| BUTTERFLY | SHASTA | BROWN EYES | PARADISE RED | PARADISE GREEN | GOLD OAK SILVER OAK WHITE OAK |

THE Lotus Glass Co. — BARNESVILLE, OHIO 43713

---

## Wildings
### a new winner by Lotus

An outdoors appeal for the sportsmen who prefer the better things of life. WILDINGS . . . the new design in 22 Karat Gold and Ebony Black Enamel on fine Crystal will be the highlight of the evening's entertainment.

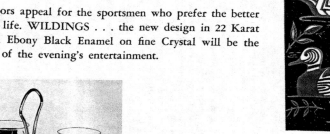

**L-4-102-14  Hi-Ball 5 piece Caddy Set ___$5.00.**
6 Sets in a Master Carton—25 Lbs.

This new heavy gauge, gold plated, center handle rack complements the beauty of the design and the pleasure of serving.

**L-8-102-14  Hi-Ball 9 piece Rack Set _____$8.00**
6 Sets in a Master Carton—45 Lbs.

| 102-14 oz. | Hi-Ball | per set of 8 | $5.50 |
| 821-14 oz. | Sky Ball | per set of 8 | 6.50 |
| 822-12 oz. | Hi-Ball | per set of 8 | 5.50 |
| 823-13 oz. | Suburban | per set of 8 | 6.50 |
| 824- 9 oz. | On the Rocks | per set of 8 | 5.50 |
| 825- 4 oz. | Cocktail | per set of 8 | 5.50 |
| L4-101-14 | Hi-Ball | 5-pc. Caddy Set | 5.00 |
| L8-102-14 | Hi-Ball | 9-pc. Rack Set | 8.00 |

| Sky Ball 821—14 oz. | Hi-Ball 822—12 oz. | Suburban 823—13 oz. | On the Rocks 824—9 oz. | Cocktail 825—4 oz. |

Prices are Retail, F.O.B., Barnesville, Ohio. No Packing Charge. Terms 1/15. Net 30.

Lotus **GLASS CO.** BOX 191  BARNESVILLE, OHIO, U.S.A.
"Creators of Fine Glassware Since 1912" If you are not listed in Dun & Bradstreet, please

PROVINCE  FLIGHT  DUCKS/DRAKES

MARSHLAND  MISTY ROSE  FRAGANCE

CARDINAL  DOWNLANS  TAHITI

THE *Lotus* Glass Co. — BARNESVILLE, OHIO 43713

| 102 – 14 OZ. QUEENS LACE | 102 – 14 OZ. DEBUTANTE ROSE | 102 – 14 OZ. 40TH ANNIVERSARY | 102 – 14 OZ. GOLD WHEAT SILVER WHEAT |

| 102 – 14 OZ. CAPRI | 102 – 14 OZ. KAHAKI | 214 – 12 OZ. PHEASANT | 102 – 14 OZ. GOLD OAK SILVER OAK WHITE OAK | 214 – 12 OZ. MALLARD | 102 – 14 OZ. BLACK GOLD |

**MIDNITE**

| 214 – 12 OZ. ICE TEA | 218 – 14 OZ. TUMBLER | 217 – 11 OZ. DBL. OLD FASHION | 216 – 8 OZ. OLD FASHION | 2967 – 11 OZ. ROLY POLY |

All items in Midnite also made in Pheasant, Northern Lights, Mallard, Provincial, Lion, Mushroom, Shasta, Brown Eyes, Galleon.

THE *Lotus* Glass Co. — BARNESVILLE, OHIO 43713

SAVOY

PAISLEY

CASTILLIAN GOLD

THE *Lotus* GLASS COMPANY
Box 191 • Barnesville, Ohio 43713

*"Creators of Fine Glassware Since 1912"*

**LATTICE**
Carmen or Emerald
with White and Gold

**KAHAKI**
Turquoise and Gold

**TEMPO**
Carmine, Emerald,
Blue or Topaz
with White and Gold

**PARADISE**
Carmen or Emerald
with White and Gold

*Lotus*

**SILVER WHEAT**
Platinum
Gold Wheat

**OAKWOOD**
White and Gold

**OAKWOOD**
Charcoal and Gold

**SILVER OAK**
Platinum
Golden Oak
Gold
White Oaks
Matte White

*Lotus*

**BON APPETITE**
White and Gold

**BON APPETITE**
Black and Gold

**FORECAST**
Black and Gold

**FLIGHT**
White and Green

**WILDLIFE**
White and Green

**BLACK GOLD**
Black and Gold

**HERITAGE**
Gold

**JUBILEE 25TH**
Platinum

**25TH ANNIVERSARY**
Platinum

*Lotus*

**CELEBRATION PLATINUM**
Carmen or Blue with
White and Platinum

**40TH ANNIVERSARY**
Ruby and Gold Band

**FROSTED ANNIVERSARY**
Gold 50th
or 25th Platinum

**CELEBRATION GOLD**
Carmen or Blue
with White and Gold

**JUBILEE 50TH**
Gold

**50TH ANNIVERSARY**
Gold

# MIDNITE

**Matte White color on Charcoal Crystal**

| 214—12 oz. | 218—14 oz. | 217—11 oz. | 209—9 oz. | 216—8 oz. | 215—5 oz. | 2967—11 oz. |
|---|---|---|---|---|---|---|
| Ice Tea | Tumbler | Dbl. Old Fashion | Juice | Old Fashion | Cocktail | Roly Poly |

—— ALL OF THESE PATTERNS ARE AVAILABLE IN ANY OF THE ABOVE SIZES ——

| 214—12 | 214—12 | 214—12 | 214—12 | 214—12 | 214—12 |
|---|---|---|---|---|---|
| Provincial | Mallard | Decoy | Pheasant | Northern Lights | Galleon |

THE *Lotus* Glass Co. — BARNESVILLE, OHIO 43713

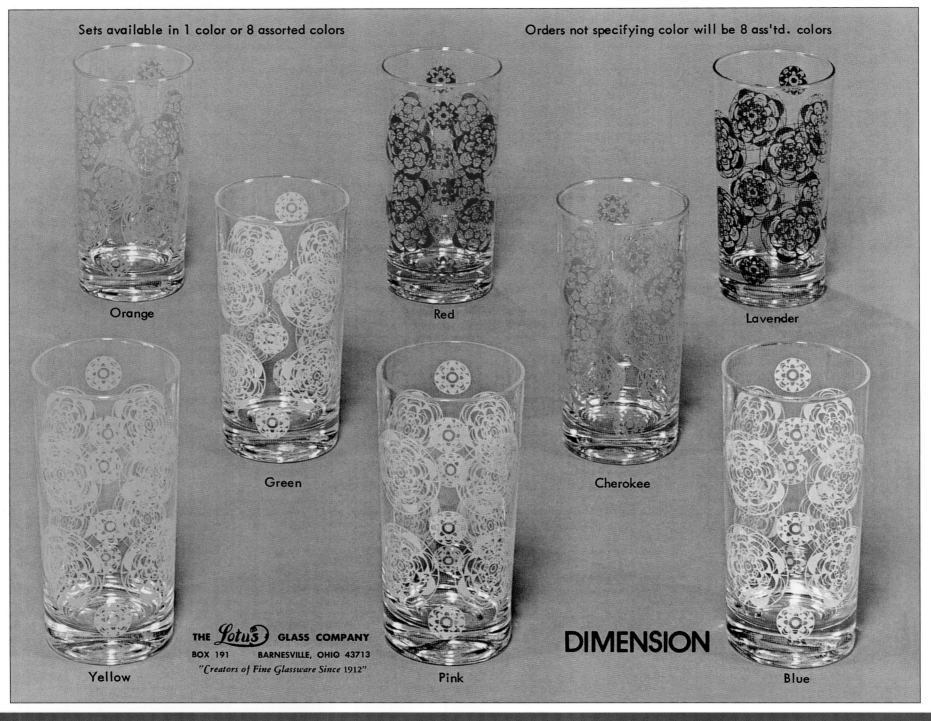

Orange

Green

Red

Lavender

Yellow

THE *Lotus* GLASS COMPANY
BOX 191    BARNESVILLE, OHIO 43713
*"Creators of Fine Glassware Since 1912"*

Pink

Cherokee

**DIMENSION**

Blue

Orders not specifying color will be 8 ass'td. colors

JEWELS

Lavender

Red

Orange

Green

Cherokee

Yellow

Pink

Blue

THE *Lotus* GLASS COMPANY
BOX 191   BARNESVILLE, OHIO 43713
*"Creators of Fine Glassware Since 1912"*

Sets available in 1 color or 8 assorted colors

| ROSE MUNDE | PHEASANT | MIDNIGHT | MALLARD | DEBUTANTE ROSE | GOLD WHEAT SILVER WHEAT |

BIRDS ASSTD. ONLY

FRUIT ASSTD. ONLY

| 828 | 102-14 | 118-14 | 117-11 | 116-8 | 115-5 |

BLACK GOLD

THE *Lotus* Glass Co. — BARNESVILLE, OHIO 43713

---

## Continental Cut Crystal

### CRYSTAL by *Lotus*

A treat for the discriminating hos[t]
Highly polished clear crystal wit[h]
heavy bottom and ground. Polishe[d]
edge fits the lip. Minimum order ca[r]
ton lots.

821—14 oz. Sky Ball
Cut 14 Flute
3 Doz. Per Carton
Wt. 23 lbs.
Per Doz. $4.80

822—12 oz. Hi-Ball
Cut 14 Flute
6 Doz. Per Carton
Wt. 41 lbs.
Per Doz. $4.20

823—13 oz.
Suburban Cut 14 Flute
3 Doz. Per Carton
Wt. 25 lbs.
Per Doz. $4.80

824—9 oz.
On the Rocks
Cut 14 Flute
6 Doz. Per Carton
Wt. 36 lbs.
Per Doz. $4.20

825—4 oz. Cocktail
Cut 14 Flute
6 Doz. Per Carton
Wt. 20 lbs.
Per Doz. $3.60

## Leo Carved Crystal

### DECORATION NO. 1020
### and Polished Fluting

821—14 oz. Sky Ball
Decor. No. 1020 & Flute
3 Doz. per ctn., Wt. 23 lbs.
Price Per Doz. $12.00

822—12 oz. Hi Ball
Decor. No. 1020 & Flute
6 Doz. per ctn., Wt. 41 lbs.
Price Per Doz. $10.80

823—13 oz. Suburban
Decor. No. 1020 & Flute
3 Doz. per ctn., Wt. 25 lbs.
Price Per Doz. $12.00

824—9 oz. On the Rocks
Decor. No. 1020 & Flute
6 Doz. per ctn., Wt. 36 lbs.
Price Per Doz. $10.80

THE

 GLASS CO.    BARNESVILLE, OHIO

"Decorators of Fine Glassware since 1912"

## Chapter Nine
# Miscellaneous Lotus Glassware

Lotus produced a wide variety of wares that are not included in this book. Some were made at the end of time at Lotus and yet lack interest for most collectors. Some of the objects shown simply do not fit easily elsewhere into the format of this book. Here are a final few illustrations of the some of the variety of decorations and forms utilized by Lotus over time, they lack any hint of market pricing because I do not believe they are traded frequently enough yet to establish any sense of secondary market value.

THE LOTUS GLASS COMPANY... BARNESVILLE, OHIO, U. S. A. [27]

LEAD BLOWN CRYSTAL GLASS

No 86 Buttercup Stemware
Decoration No. 0116GB
22 Karat Gold

No 71 Royal Windsor Encrusted Stemware
Decoration No. 124
22 Karat Gold

No 86 Gold Band Stemware
Decoration "B"
22 Karat Gold

No 86 Platinum Stemware
Decoration: Platinum "E"

## THE LOTUS GLASS COMPANY, Barnesville, Ohio 43713
### Hurricane Lamps and Candelabra With Imported
### Hand Cut & Polished Glass Prisms

Bridal Bouquet 0906
1947—10¾ in.—1 Lite
Hurricane Lamp Complete
6 Hand Cut & Polished Prisms
Plate Etched 278—5½ Shade
& Base

Bridal Bouquet C906
1948—10½ in.—2 Lite
Hurricane Lamp Complete
12 Hand Cut & Polished Prisms
Plate Etched 278—5½ Shade
& Base

Prelude 1042
1947—10¾ in.—1 Lite
Hurricane Lamp Complete
6 Hand Cut & Polished Prisms
Plate Etched 278—5½ Base
& Shade

Prelude 1042
1947—10½ in.—2 Lite
Hurricane Lamp Complete
12 Hand Cut & Polished Prisms
Plate Etched 278—5½ Shade
& Base

Sizes given are overall measurements for completed lamps.                    Wax Candles are not furnished.

## THE LOTUS GLASS COMPANY, Barnesville, Ohio 43713
### Hurricane Lamps and Candelabra With Imported
### Hand Cut & Polished Glass Prisms

Polished Cut 62½ York
1947—10¾ in.—1 Lite
Hurricane Lamp Complete
6 Hand Cut & Polished Crystal
Prisms with 278—5½ Shade
Polished Cut Base & Shade

Polished York 62½
1948—10½ in.—2 Lite
Hurricane Lamp Complete
12 Hand Cut & Polished Prisms
278—5½ Base
& Shade

Gray Cut 96½
1947—10¾ in.—1 Lite
Hurricane Lamp Complete
6 Hand Cut & Polished Crystal
Prisms with 278—5½ Shade
Gray Cut Base & Shade

Gray Cut 96½
1948—10½ in.—2 Lite
Hurricane Lamp Complete
12 Hand Cut & Polished Prisms
Gray Cut 278—5½ Shade
Gray Cut Base

Sizes given are overall measurements for completed lamps.                    Wax Candles are not furnished.

# *1776 – 1976*

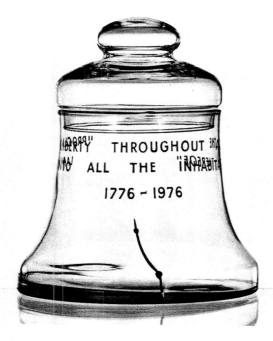

LIBERTY BELL
949 COVD. CANDY
$4.25 EACH

AMERICAN
102-14 TUMBLER
$3.50 SET OF 8

AMERICAN
924 CANDY JAR
$2.25 EACH

AMERICAN
949 COVD. CANDY
$4.25 EACH

THE

Lotus

**GLASS CO.** BOX 191 BARNESVILLE, OHIO, U.S.A. 43713

*"Creators of Fine Glassware Since 1912"*

If you are not listed in Dun & Bradstreet, please
enclose check for the full amount of the order.
All orders under $25 will carry 20% handling
charge.

# WHITE FROST

. . . the overall delicate tracery on our handblown crystal captures the crisp, frosty look of the indescribably beautiful ice crystal designs that pattern window-panes in winter —captivating the imagination.

No. 82—10"    No. 82—8"    No. 82—6"

*"Creators of Fine Glassware since 1912"*

Lotus

197
Comport

926
Candy

940—Small
941—Medium
942—Large

## Lotus Golden Wedding Gifts Lotus

### HAND MADE 22 KARAT GOLD HAND DECORATED---GOLD DECORATORS SINCE 1912

Produced only by Lotus craftsmen with whom quality gold has been a tradition, decorating on the lovely shapes and finest blanks. Makes a combination of practical gift items at a price that your most exacting price conscious customer will appreciate.

41-6    96-6    830-9¼    832-7½    56-6    34-8

95-5    43-5    94-4    2-5    393-4

2-4½    93-3    36    13-3¼

39-10    81-10    83-10    83-6    81-6    82-6    84-6    32-8    172-10    82-10

THE Lotus GLASS CO.    BOX 191   BARNESVILLE, OHIO, U.S.A. 43713

*"Creators of Fine Glassware Since 1912"*

If you are not listed in Dun & Bradstreet, please enclose check for the full amount of the order. All orders under $25 will carry 20% handling charge.

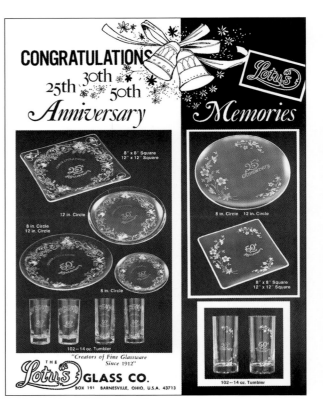

# CONGRATULATIONS
## 25th 30th 50th Anniversary

Lotus

## Memories

8" x 8" Square
12" x 12" Square

12 in. Circle

8 in. Circle
12 in. Circle

12 in. Circle

8 in. Circle

8 in. Circle   12 in. Circle

8" x 8" Square
12" x 12" Square

102—14 oz. Tumbler

*"Creators of Fine Glassware Since 1912"*

THE Lotus GLASS CO.
BOX 191  BARNESVILLE, OHIO, U.S.A. 43713

102—14 oz. Tumbler

# Replacements LTD. &
# West Virginia Museum of American Glass

Archival material, including several Lotus catalogs, are to be found at the West Virginia Museum of American Glass(WVMAG). WVMAG is a major resource for information on twentieth century American Glass. The extensive hot glass manufacturers catalog collection held by the museum may be found on line at http:members.aol.com/wvmuseumofglass/ and photocopies of any catalog may be ordered. The holdings of glass decorators' catalogs, as well as those of importers and others related to glass, may be searched and copied on site.

WVMAG is one of the few sites dedicated to preserving and displaying popular twentieth century American glass in its many forms. The Museum publishes a popular magazine for glass collectors and students called *All About Glass* (www.allaboutglass.org) and presents an active program of exhibitions, seminars, and other preservation and educational activities.

Replacements, LTD. is the world's largest supplier of active and discontinued china, crystal, flatware, and collectables. Within that extensive list of offerings falls Lotus glass. At the time I write this Replacements, LTD. has catalogued within their data base well over 600 Lotus and Glastonbury/Lotus patterns. Recall that their specialty will be in helping you with stemware and serving pieces for the table, but some giftware may be found. Should you desire replacements for use or additions to your collection, I confidently suggest contacting Replacements, LTD via their web site at www.replacements.com or by calling 1-800-737-5223.

# Bibliography

Bredehoft, Neila and Tom. *Heisey Glass. 1896-1957*. Paducah, Kentucky: Collector Books, 2001.

Comins, Linda. "A Cut Above: Barnesville Company Glass Once Used by Hotels, State Department, Congress." *Wheeling News-Register*, 18 August 1996.

Domitz, Carrie. *Paden City Glass Identification and Values*. Paducah, Kentucky: Collector Books, 2004.

Felt, Tom and Elaine and Rich Stoer. *The Candlestick Book Vol. 1*. Paducah, Kentucky: Collector Books, 2003.

Felt, Tom and Elaine and Rich Stoer. *The Candlestick Book Vol. 2*. Paducah, Kentucky: Collector Books, 2003.

Hanse, Don. Interviews, photographs, and papers shared from family collection.

Krause, Gail. *The Encyclopedia of Duncan Glass*. Hicksville, New York: Exposition Press, 1976.

Long, Milbra and Emily Seate. *Fostoria Tableware 1924-1943 The Crystal for America*. Paducah, Kentucky: Collector Books, 1999.

Ionne, Joe. "A Touch Of Gold." *Columbus Dispatch Sunday Magazine*, 8 July 1973.

Kovar, Lorraine. *Westmoreland Glass Volume 3 1888-1940*. Marietta, Ohio: Glass Press, 1997.

Lotus Glass. Various company catalogs and fliers.

Murphy, Fran. "The Bells Are Ringing." *Akron Beacon Journal*, 21 August 1975.

National Cambridge Glass Collectors, Inc. *Fine Handmade Table Glassware 1949-1953 by the Cambridge Glass Co. 1949-1953*. Paducah Kentucky: Collector Books, 1978.

Page, Bob and Dale Fredericksen. *A Collection of American Crystal: A Stemware Identification Guide for Glastonebury Lotus, Libbey/Rock Sharpe & Hawkes*. Greensboro, North Carolina: Page-Fredericksen Publishing Co., 1995.

Schmidt, Tim. *Central Glass Works. The Depression Era*. Atglen, Pennsylvania: Schiffer Publishing, 2004.

Six, Dean. *West Virginia Glass Between the World Wars*. Atglen, Pennsylvania: Schiffer Publishing, 2002.

Yarnall, Bruce. "Glass Decorating Firm Suspends Production." *Barnesville Enterprise*, 10 January 1996.

Weatherman, Hazel Marie. *Colored Glassware of the Depression Era 2*. Ozark, Missouri: Glassbooks, 1974.

Wilson, Charles West. *Westmoreland Glass*. Paducah, Kentucky: Collector Books, 1996.

## Periodicals

*Pottery, Glass & Brass Salesman, The*
*Crockery and Glass Journal, The*
*Keystone, The*

# Index